MW00510750

THE ECOSYSTEM ECONOMY

HOW TO LEAD IN THE NEW AGE OF SECTORS WITHOUT BORDERS

THE ECOSYSTEM ECONOMY

HOW TO LEAD IN THE NEW AGE OF SECTORS WITHOUT BORDERS

Venkat Atluri and
Miklós Dietz

WILEY

Published by John Wiley & Sons, Inc., Hoboken, New Jersey.
Published simultaneously in Canada.

For general information on our other products and services or for technical support, please contact our Customer Care Department within the United States at (800) 762-2974, outside the United States at (317) 572-3993 or fax (317) 572-4002.

Wiley also publishes its books in a variety of electronic formats. Some content that appears in print may not be available in electronic formats. For more information about Wiley products, visit our web site at www.wiley.com.

Library of Congress Cataloging-in-Publication Data is Available:

ISBN 9781119984788 (Hardback)
ISBN 9781119984801 (ePDF)
ISBN 9781119984795 (ePub)

Cover Design: Wiley
Cover Image: (Frame) Wiley, (Pencil) © LUHUANFENG/Getty Images

SKY10035142_082322

Contents

Introduction

The Age of Ecosystems: Taking Stock of a Transformation in Progress

The future has never seemed more exciting or more confusing. When we look outside today, we are confronted with a multitude of exhilarating, sometimes vexing, and vitally important trends unfolding in the realms of culture, business, and technology. For the uninitiated, it all might seem overwhelming: cryptocurrencies, artificial intelligence, Web 3.0, quantum computing, automated cars, the internet of things, smart homes, and biomedical miracles. The list goes on and on. What it adds up to is a kaleidoscope of overlapping, cataclysmic changes all happening at once, each of which carries the potential to transform the world—and each of which is probably complex enough in its own right to spend a whole book contemplating.

However, if we take a deeper look—if we cut through the noise—we can see something else. On closer examination, almost all of these dizzying developments unfolding in the world today are related to another phenomenon altogether. The phenomenon is this: the borders between the traditional sectors of our economy are fading away. We're used to thinking about the economy in terms of sectors like construction, real estate, information technology, automotive manufacturing, energy, financial services, and health care—to name just a few. We've always understood these sectors to be discrete categories, and each has traditionally operated in its own sphere. But now, the economy is changing on a fundamental level. And as the borders between sectors blur, new organizing structures are forming in their place. If this seems like an abstraction to you, consider this: many businesses are already starting to adapt. This is more than just a theory—it's actually happening.

The transition away from sectors is such a fundamental change, it can be difficult to wrap our minds around. We are facing one of the biggest market shifts in economic history. For our whole lives, we've understood our economy in terms of sectors. As we'll see in Chapter 1, the concept has been around for thousands of years. It seemed like the lines dividing sectors were carved into the very bedrock of the marketplace—they were considered not only real and tangible, but inescapable. Now, that is changing. Sectors are becoming a less and less compelling way of describing the economy because, increasingly, the borders between them are dissolving. Why is this? We'll spend a significant part of this book exploring this question, but for now, it will have to suffice to say that in the early twenty-first century, we hit a turning point that made it possible for businesses to ignore these borders and do something new—in the true interest of delivering value for all.

What does this mean? In short, for many businesses, everything is changing: their customers, their competitors, their business models. They will have to reinvent themselves to operate in an entirely different environment. As the borders between sectors fade, businesses are organizing into new, more dynamic configurations, centered not on the way things have always been done, but on people's needs. These new formations are what we call ecosystems: communities of interconnected digital and physical businesses that work across traditional sector boundaries to provide customers with everything they could want related to a particular need or set of needs, whether it's housing, health, or entertainment. Businesses form ecosystems by collaborating with one another—by sharing assets, information, and resources—and ultimately creating value beyond what would have been possible for each of them to achieve individually. These business are doing more than just finding new ways to slice the pie—by working together, and working across industry boundaries, they are creating value propositions that actually expand the pie, that accomplish more collectively than each can individually. Because each business that takes part in an ecosystem contributes to this collective process of value creation, each also shares in the upside that is generated. The result is a dynamic, creative, powerful new kind of business formation that stands to transform the economy as we know it (Figure I.1).

FIGURE I.1 **Definition of an ecosystem**

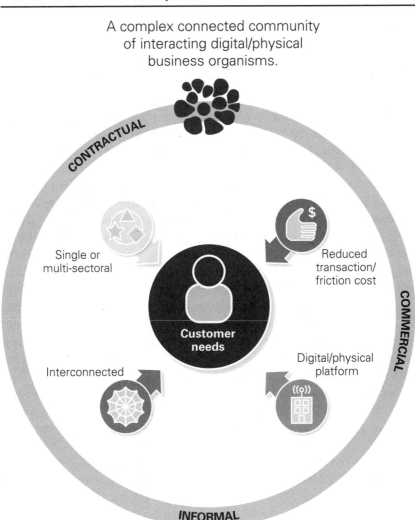

A complex connected community
of interacting digital/physical
business organisms.

CONTRACTUAL

COMMERCIAL

Single or
multi-sectoral

Reduced
transaction/
friction cost

Customer
needs

Digital/physical
platform

Interconnected

INFORMAL

Why do we use the word *ecosystem* to describe this sort of community? When we're talking about the natural world, we often use the word to mean a community of biological organisms that are interdependent, or which together form a web of symbiotic relationships that meet the particular needs of each organism. In a forest ecosystem, for example, we can imagine how this web would look: bears eat the deer, while the deer eat plants that are fertilized by the bears' droppings, as well as decomposed leaves and other vegetation. The vegetation is converted into soil by worms, which are eaten by birds, which also eat small rodents, which subsist on tree nuts, which are sustained by the soil and the decomposing vegetation. Each organism is dependent on the web that connects them all. Similarly, businesses can come together to create webs of mutually beneficial relationships centered on meeting customers' needs. The analogy is far from perfect—of course, there are many differences between the workings of business ecosystems and natural ecosystems—but the core concept is similar enough to be instructive.

Chances are you've heard the term *ecosystem* thrown around quite a bit in a business context. The concept is widely recognized. Somewhat counterintuitively, this poses a bit of a problem. Because it is so frequently discussed and so commonly cited, there is a lack of clarity about its real meaning—and in many cases, people use the term to mean something much more limited and less meaningful than what we have in mind. There are CEOs today who will look at their traditional vendor and client relationships and fool themselves into thinking that this constitutes an ecosystem. When we use the term in this book, we use it to refer to much deeper connections between businesses—alliances that are about collectively creating and sharing value in the best interests of the customer.

To better understand how and why businesses form these ecosystems, consider the supermarket. When we speak of ecosystems today, our thoughts tend toward high-tech businesses. But these companies have non-digital precursors from decades before the rise of the internet that illustrate the same core concept. Before the rise of supermarkets, families purchased their food from a wide range of different specialized vendors. Milk was delivered by a milkman; fish came from a fishmonger; meat from a butcher; produce from a greengrocer; rice, beans, and other staples from a dry goods store. The innovation of the supermarket was to combine each of these previously separate functions into a single, comprehensive, one-stop source for all grocery needs. Rather than being organized by supply chain, as the older, specialty shops were, the supermarket was organized according to customer needs. Customers did not *want* to visit five to ten different vendors in order to do their shopping for the week—they did so because it was the only way they had ever known, and it was the only way to get the items they needed. It was the way food distribution had developed over years and years. What people truly wanted was simplicity—a one-stop shopping experience. As soon as the supermarket was introduced, it quickly became the dominant form.[1]

Today, with a big push from new technological advances, businesses are increasingly coming together to form comprehensive ecosystems that similarly cater to multiple needs simultaneously—essentially replicating the supermarket effect on a much larger scale. These pioneers are using digital platforms (both hardware and software) to spur innovation by organizing businesses into new collaborative formations like app stores and digital marketplaces with innovative economic models. Think of a company like Rakuten, in Japan, which offers loans, credit cards, fintech, travel booking, instant messaging, and food delivery. Or a company like Amazon in the United States, which offers music, video, gaming, cloud computing, supermarkets, and online retail. Or still others, like Apple, Tencent, Alibaba, or Google. Here's a challenge: try to identify a single sector that each of these companies belongs to.

It is an impossible task. The reason is that these are ecosystem businesses—and as such, they span multiple sectors. In fact, they are organized in a way that completely disregards the traditional borders between sectors. Of course, another kind of sector-spanning company has been commonplace for ages: the conglomerate. You might wonder how ecosystem companies differ from conglomerates. We'll tackle this question more fully in Chapter 1, but for now, the short answer is that ecosystems are centered on customer needs—whereas conglomerates are not necessarily. As we'll see, there are different ways of being an ecosystem player. Some involve collaborating with select partners to build your business across sector borders in order to meet customer needs in a particular category or set of categories. Others involve working closely with many partners or facilitating a large platform on which other players can come together. The core concept, though, is that players are crossing sector borders in the service of meeting a set of customer needs *holistically*.

To illustrate how ecosystems work, let's consider a few that are already making waves in the world today. For example, imagine an ecosystem focused on fulfilling customers' needs in the category of health. Think of the typical steps a person might take as they go about maintaining their health—choosing and managing a health insurance policy, receiving preventative care, getting prescriptions filled, choosing wellness activities like a fitness class, or services like a diet tracker—even receiving major treatments like a surgery, and managing the resulting insurance claims and bills. Together, these steps constitute the customer's journey; the idea of an ecosystem is to bring them all together—or rather, to bring as many of them together as possible. Even if each step in that journey is fulfilled or managed by a different company, the ecosystem integrates them into a single platform, so that from the customer's perspective, it's all one experience, one journey. Ecosystems are particularly effective—and attractive to customers—when they are able to solve critical pain points with tailored solutions. In other words, if an ecosystem can help consumers through the most arduous step on their journey, they will be more likely to trust the broader ecosystem with the rest of their needs. At no time was this clearer than in 2020, at the beginning of the COVID-19 pandemic, when millions and millions of patients experienced a new pain point—the inability to safely leave one's home to conduct routine business, like going to a doctor's office. This led to the rapid and widespread adoption of a service that had previously been considered very niche: telehealth. And as they adopted telehealth, consumers also became generally much more open to the idea of getting health care through ecosystem-based providers.

But there are many other fundamental needs that can form the basis of an ecosystem. If the core need we're talking about is, say, the need for a home, the story would be a bit different. A home ecosystem would involve multiple companies coming together to meet every need a consumer might have in the process of obtaining and maintaining a home. Anyone who has been through that process, especially in recent years, knows how much of a headache it can be. It begins with the search, so an essential component of a home ecosystem may be a real estate and rental search engine like Zillow. Other needs include financing, insurance, inspection, appraisal, moving, renovation, legal issues, upkeep, and maintenance. If we were to imagine a comprehensive home ecosystem, it would incorporate each of these—whether through a series of partnerships or through a digital platform that connects services from different companies into a single, integrated experience. In either case, the end result for users would be a one-stop shop for everything home-related, from searching, to buying, to decorating, to maintaining—all the way to selling, when it's time to move and begin the cycle all over again. Throughout all of it, customer needs come first.

To take a slightly different example, let's think about businesses' needs as well as peoples'. Businesses, after all, are run by people, and are likewise attracted to the prospect of having all their needs fulfilled in the same place. One business need that has become the basis for an ecosystem, for example, is the need for business-to-business (B2B) services. Think of the typical operations services that small and medium enterprises (SMEs) might need help with: getting funding, managing finances, marketing (including digital advertising), IT infrastructure, legal advice, office management, and human resources. One commonality that unites almost all entrepreneurs is that they prefer to spend as little time on these tasks as possible. A B2B services or small business ecosystem, then, would be focused on delivering as many of these needs as possible for SMEs all together, perhaps through an all-inclusive digital platform.

Hopefully, by now the power of ecosystems is becoming clear. Once established, successful ecosystems create a virtuous cycle that fuels their growth. By offering products and services that individual companies could not create as effectively on their own, ecosystems draw in more and more customers and ultimately generate a network effect. More customers mean more data, which companies can leverage to fashion even better offerings, which in turn further improves the companies' processes and wins more customers. As ecosystems bridge openings along the value chain, they create a customer-centric, unified value proposition in which users can enjoy an end-to-end experience for a wide range of products and services through a single access gateway. Along the way, customers' costs go down even as they gain new experiences, all of which whets their appetite for more.

The stakes could not be higher. To understand why, try this: look up the top ten companies worldwide today in terms of market capitalization, then compare the list to the top ten companies a decade ago, or two decades ago. The lists will look completely different, of course, and that's to be expected—after all, times change. But if you take a closer look, you will notice something curious. In the past, this list was dominated by companies that were easy to classify—in other words, by non-ecosystem players: oil and gas companies like ExxonMobil, insurers like AIG, and financial institutions like Citi. Today, although the list remains constantly in flux, you are likely to find that a significant majority of those top ten companies are ecosystem players—companies that defy easy categorization because they work in concert with a community of partners to create value propositions that span sector boundaries. Among them, you are almost certain to see Apple, Microsoft, Alphabet, Amazon, and Meta.[2] How would you classify these companies? To say they're tech companies would be an oversimplification. Apple offers credit cards and runs the App Store, which provides customers with everything from food delivery to exercise classes to ride sharing. Amazon runs a large chain of grocery stores and owns the movie studio MGM.

The difference between the list of top companies in years past and today reflects a colossal economic reorientation, the significance of which is only now beginning to be felt. Already, capital markets are betting untold trillions of dollars on these ecosystem companies. But the enormous powers they currently wield today are just the tip of the iceberg. We believe that in the coming decades, the fundamental structure of the global economy will be recast into an entirely new shape. This carries a number of important consequences, the most significant being that a nearly incomprehensible amount of value is at stake. According to a recent analysis, this new breed of multi-sectoral, category-defying ecosystem companies—which comprise what we call the integrated network economy—could reach roughly one third of global gross economic output (measured in revenues) over the next few decades. That's about $70–100 trillion (see Figure I.2).[3]

If you are interested in getting a piece of that $70–100 trillion, you will need to understand the fundamentals of the massive transformation currently taking place—which is exactly what this book aims to help you do. In the pages that follow, we will explain why this transformation is happening, why it's happening now, how it is likely to

FIGURE I.2   **In the coming decades the emerging ecosystem economy could drive $70 to $100 trillion of revenue**

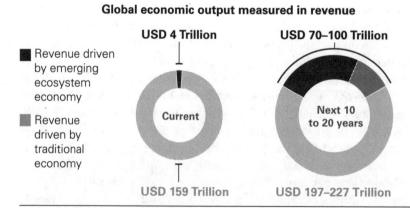

Global economic output measured in revenue

■ Revenue driven by emerging ecosystem economy

■ Revenue driven by traditional economy

USD 4 Trillion — Current — USD 159 Trillion

USD 70–100 Trillion — Next 10 to 20 years — USD 197–227 Trillion

Sources: McKinsey analysis, IHS World Industry Service.

continue unfolding in the decades ahead, and—most importantly—what you should do about it.

If the $70–100 trillion isn't enough to convince you, perhaps this will be: you don't have a choice. This integrated ecosystem economy is coming whether you are ready or not—in fact, it's already here—and failing to act would be an enormous missed opportunity. There is a new set of rules, a new set of incentives—a whole new game to play. Continuing to play by the old rules will mean not only missing out on the rewards of the ecosystem economy, but facing disintermediation, disaggregation, commoditization, and invisibility—what we call the four horsemen of the apocalypse. The ecosystem economy opens enormous opportunities for creative business offerings, but also brings great danger.

The upshot is that no one is safe. Most of today's big ecosystem players got their start by using technological advances to create new digital versions of businesses that had previously been conducted offline. In the process, they built a strong foundation from which to launch ecosystem-oriented businesses. But increasingly, as ecosystems become a more dominant force in our economic life, and as the barriers between sectors continue to fade away, we are seeing an incredible breadth of ecosystem plays. New attacks will come not only from tech companies disrupting physical businesses—they could come from any direction: large established companies leveraging their data and assets to break into new areas, agile upstarts taking advantage of new technologies or regulatory changes, and companies you never in your wildest dreams would have expected to compete against. In short, incumbents aren't incumbents anymore. In fact, the very notion of incumbency is no longer relevant. Every company in the world, big and small, is going to have to gear up for a new kind of fight.

If this sounds scary, that's because it should. To have any hope of surviving and flourishing in the coming decades, you will need completely new ways of thinking, new ways of formulating strategies, and new ways of executing them. The rules of this fight are entirely novel. For centuries and centuries, the basic organizing principle of discrete sectors remained a constant—and that basic fact touched every other aspect of economic life around the world. But now that is changing. To win at this new game, in this new, hypercompetitive economy, business leaders are going to need entirely new philosophies and new playbooks. The purpose of this book is to explain why these changes are happening, and to give you the understanding and knowledge you need to navigate the new economy they are producing.

Let's be very clear about this: there is no one tool that can prepare us for the ecosystem economy. We can't delegate ecosystem transformations to a chief data officer (CDO) alone, or to a chief marketing officer (CMO) or to a chief technology officer (CTO) or to any other single department. The ecosystem economy demands that we rework our entire approach to competition, and that we do it as a team—from the board and the CEO on down. It requires that we transform our organizations on a most basic level—that we rethink who we are as a company, where we compete, who we partner with, what value propositions we offer, how we execute our plays, how we create value in the broader ecosystem economy, and how we capture some of that value. This book will give you the tools you need to find meaningful, actionable answers to those questions.

Because the coming of ecosystems is so transformative and so important, we want to be as direct as possible in telling you about them. For that reason, this book's organization is simple. The book is divided into two parts.

In Part One, we will tell you about the past, present, and future of ecosystems. We will explain how humanity finally began to break away from sectors; how a confluence of changing consumer patterns and technology breakthroughs created some of the first ecosystems; and how, in the coming decades, ecosystems will turn the world inside out before our eyes. In other words: Why is this happening? Why is it happening now? And where do we think these changes are taking us? In Part Two, we will explore the real-world implications of these momentous changes—and give you all the knowledge you need to adapt and stay ahead of the shifting landscape, whether you're a CEO, an upstart entrepreneur, an MBA student, or anywhere in between. We will explain, in short, why these changes have created totally new rules of the game.

The economy, of course, is always changing—and always has been. At many points in the past, during times of great upheaval or difficult transition, perceptive and forward-thinking businesspeople have been able to stay ahead of their competitors by skillfully reading the signs and preempting the changes they herald. We hope our book will be able to help you do something similar in the years ahead—but this time, keeping ahead of the curve is even more important. The transformation we are witnessing now is not merely the next in a series of ordinary rearrangements—it is the biggest and most consequential economic change in recent history. There is simply no other option but to make sure you are ready.

As we said at the outset, we are all living through a time of chaotic transformations at every level of society. These changes can be difficult to interpret and even more challenging to act on. But finding a way to make sense of them is vital. At its heart, this book's purpose is to cut through the noise and offer clarity in the face of these often-confounding developments—to zoom out and show the bigger picture. For it is only by doing so that we can find a way to thrive in the coming ecosystem economy.

Part One

1

Sparks of Magic

The Road from Sectors
to Earliest Ecosystems

Let's start by going all the way back to the beginning—to humanity's earliest days, thousands and thousands of years ago. Back then, humans were nomadic bands of hunter-gatherers striving for basic subsistence, only slightly more capable than the hominids from the opening scenes of *2001: A Space Odyssey* who discover the use of tools. Life was, as Thomas Hobbes famously put it in his *Leviathan*, "nasty, brutish, and short."[1]

Think of everything that has happened since then. Humans developed agriculture and founded permanent settlements. We domesticated animals, learned to make metal, built cities, and developed sophisticated societies with thriving political and artistic cultures.[2] The human lifespan tripled. The difference between what life was for humans then and what it is now is staggering—it is incalculable. And yet, if we look closely, we will see that there is one thing that has remained relatively unchanged over all these years—from the very beginning of organized work until very recently: this whole time, humans have been organizing their work into discrete categories that essentially functioned as sectors of the economy.

As civilization grew more advanced and thus more complex, people needed work to be more organized and efficient. The result was that, over time, the boundaries between these categories gradually became more and more delineated. When humans were nomadic hunter-gatherers, it made sense for work to be generalized. But as civilizations started to grow and flourish, people found they could accomplish more with less effort if they specialized and divided their work into separate designations. So, for example, the work of brickmaking was conducted separately from the work of shipbuilding—just as the work of laying roads was separate from the work of farming, which was separate from the work of building dwellings or making pots. Each line of work was its own distinct activity, carried out by distinct practitioners who developed their work into an institution of sorts. As civilization continued to develop, differentiated forms of work became more sophisticated, more specialized, and more communal. In ancient Rome, they became formalized with the creation of what were called collegia, or professional associations. There was, for example, a college of woodworkers, a college of merchant mariners, a college of wine dealers, and a college of planters. In ancient China, a similar system developed. By the Middle Ages, guilds, a similar type of organization, had taken hold throughout much of Europe.[3]

By the time of the Industrial Revolution, in the late eighteenth and early nineteenth centuries, different industrial sectors as we think of them today had begun to form. There was, for example, a mining industry, and a textile manufacturing industry, and a glassmaking industry. Each had its own supply chains, its own forms of craftsmanship and expertise, its own specialized labor practices, and its own proprietary distribution. These differentiated industries didn't appear out of nowhere—rather, they followed the same pattern that had been set by the guilds, and the collegia before them, and the specialized lines of work going back as long as humans had been doing organized work to create value.

But that's not to say that nothing changed. Over these thousands of years of history, there was a continuous, gentle, and slow evolution: borders between these industries shifted. From time to time, certain industries no longer made sense and were eliminated. Think of the telegraph industry after the invention of the telephone. Other times, sectors would morph or merge or split; companies or organizations that were doing one kind of work would branch into others when technological advances made it easy and efficient to do so, or they would stop doing other kinds of work when someone else was able to do it better. At the same time, other sectors emerged that were newly needed because of the increasing sophistication of society or newly possible because of technological breakthroughs. Take, for example, the automotive industry, which coalesced in the late nineteenth and early twentieth centuries as engineers refined and improved the internal combustion engine. Or the computer and information technology industry, which began to take off starting in the 1970s, with the proliferation of the personal computer and new advances in the field of microelectronics.[4] But by and large, even as old industries fell and new ones arose, these categories were distinct and stayed distinct.

Now, thanks to a confluence of developments, this is finally changing. We'll explore why in the next chapter, but for the time being, what is important to understand is that sometime in the early twenty-first century, the borders between sectors started blurring. As we mentioned in the introduction, new formations called ecosystems are now taking their place. Businesses are coming together into dynamic communities that cooperatively create value by working across traditional sector boundaries.

While all of this is incredibly consequential, it's also true that—in some ways, at least—the emerging ecosystem economy may not seem so novel. After all, industry definitions have always been fluid: for centuries, really, technological developments have prompted sectors of the economy to appear, disappear, and merge. Banking, for example, was born from the merger of money exchange, merchant banking, savings banking, and safety-deposit services. Supermarkets, as we mentioned earlier, emerged by combining the previously separate functions of butchers, dairies, fishmongers, greengrocers, and others under one umbrella where customers could get all of the grocery items they needed. Over time, changes such as these created new competitors, shifted vast amounts of wealth, and reshaped significant parts of the economy. Though they happened long before the term *disruptive* was in vogue, it could be fairly applied to these shifts.

All of this might lead a person to ask: Do ecosystems really represent such a radical break from the past? Is the new business world really that different from the old? The truth is that while we have seen flickers in decades past of the magic that ecosystems can work, what we have witnessed in recent years (and are still witnessing) is something truly new and special. The ongoing digital revolution, which has been reducing frictional transaction costs for years, has accelerated as the twenty-first century has worn on, and is on the verge of triggering massive economic changes on a scale not yet seen.

To understand the importance of this new ecosystem economy and how to take on the challenges it poses, we must first understand how it differs from the economy that preceded it—that is to say, we need to understand the beliefs and assumptions that have been guiding us all this time. It is important, therefore, that we take a moment to look back at the economic history that led us to this moment, the history of how we have evolved from a sector-based economy to an ecosystem-based economy.

Sectors, of course, are groups of businesses that together occupy the same segment of the economy and offer raw materials, goods, or services within the same category. These sectors, or industries, are all around us. (Though opinions vary as to the difference between sectors and industries, we will use the terms interchangeably here.) It's not difficult to think of some examples: farming, automotive, hospitality, financial, education—the list goes on and on. What is happening now is that these categories are losing their meaning as businesses form new communities that reach across traditional sector boundaries.

As we'll explore in Part Two of this book, surviving the transition from the traditional, sector-based economy to a new ecosystem-based economy will require a significant shift in the way you think about your business. In the old world of sectors, you typically measured your success in terms of sectoral market share and relative profitability—the goal was to own the largest possible slice of your industry. Within the emerging world of ecosystems, the goal is to own your customers, to follow and guide them on their journey and build a model that serves their needs at critical junctures.

The difficulty is that industries and their borders have been with us for so long that they have become deeply engrained in our thinking—a fundamental part of how we understand the world. Indeed, they are important to everyone, not just as a frame that economists and business leaders use to inform their analyses and decisions. Most industries have worked explicitly to create a community around their common purpose and line of business—with industry conferences, industry forums, industry publications, newsletters, meetings, even shared norms and ethical practices. For many workers today, their industry and the community that surrounds it are hugely important parts of their lives. The upshot of all of this is that even though we're increasingly living in a world where traditional sectors of the economy are blurring, we seldom stop to ponder the fact of their existence. Or to consider what their absence might look like.

THE RISE OF CONGLOMERATES

As we try to understand the evolution of the ecosystem economy, it may be helpful to consider the history of a related (but importantly distinct) kind of business: conglomerates, or firms made up of multiple unrelated (or only loosely related) lines of business. As the economy became more and more complex over the years, companies and organizations expanded—and many started to branch out more and more, taking on new areas that were beyond the scope of what they originally set out to do. Other conglomerates formed by consolidating several different businesses together under one common owner. As the Nobel prize-winning economist Ronald Coase pointed out, the reason companies exist is to cut down on transaction costs—and in many cases, such savings proved attractive enough to warrant bringing together an extremely varied collection of business activities under one corporate roof.[5] This was the impulse that gave rise to conglomerates.

One of the earliest examples of this sort of sector-spanning conglomerate was the Dutch East India Company. Founded in 1602, the company, known by its initials in Dutch, VOC (for Vereenigde Oostindische Compagnie), existed for almost 200 years. As the historian Stephen Bown writes, by the late seventeenth century, the VOC was "the most powerful and richest company in the world" and was "involved in a multitude of commercial activities, such as construction, sugar refining, cloth manufacturing, tobacco curing, weaving, glass making, distilling, brewing, and other industries."[6] Whereas many later conglomerates would form as individual families or business groups accumulated more wealth and power, the formation of the VOC was directed by the Dutch government. At the time, roughly 20 Dutch syndicates had been competing to import goods such as nutmeg and cloves from Southeast Asia. The Dutch government, worried that too much competition among these groups would drive down profits, worked out an arrangement to consolidate the rivals into a single company to which it granted a government charter and a monopoly on the spice trade.[7] Although the VOC was a monopoly in this sense, its primary purpose was still to integrate various different lines of business across sector boundaries.

Before long, with its massive size and exclusive access, the company was dominating trade to the region—and, like its latter-day conglomerate descendants, it was branching into new areas in an effort to diversify its operations and revenue sources. In its effort to establish the Dutch as the undisputed worldwide leader in the spice trade, the Dutch government gave the company a broad set of powers, permitting it to make its own treaties, establish fortified outposts, and command its own army.[8] By the 1700s, the company had undergone a series of changes, gradually morphing from a corporate entity into something more resembling a state or an empire. At the same time, the margins on the VOC's most important export fell. This, combined with social and political changes in Europe, and poor management, gradually put the company on a downward trajectory, which culminated in the Dutch government revoking its charter in 1799.

In subsequent years, conglomerates continued to evolve. It wasn't until the twentieth century, however, that the circumstances arose in the US for the conglomerate to become a common and widespread form of corporate organization. In the early years of that century, a series of developments unfolded that created an ideal environment for conglomerates. According to a scholarly article on their rise and fall in the US, companies such as DuPont and General Motors in the 1920s "pioneered the use of the multi-divisional form (or M-form) to produce and market a number of related products through separate divisions." The multi-divisional structure "allowed easy integration of acquired businesses, which enabled firms to grow through acquisition." But after congress passed an antitrust law known as the Celler-Kefauver Act in 1950, "horizontal and vertical acquisitions (buying competitors, buyers, or suppliers) fell out of regulatory favor, and firms seeking to grow through acquisition were forced to diversify into other industries."[9]

This led to a period of frenzied mergers and acquisitions in the 1960s and 70s, which included the establishment of multinational conglomerate entities, such as the International Telephone & Telegraph Company (ITT), Litton Industries, Textron, and Gulf & Western. The boom was also helped by an environment of low interest rates and a somewhat turbulent, up-and-down market: companies had plenty of opportunities to buy other companies that had fallen on hard times, and they had access to easy financing thanks to the low interest rates.

As a study in the *Journal of Business and Technology Law* explains, conglomerate activity dominated during this period: "In 1968, at the height of the wave, about eighty-four percent of the large mergers were of the conglomerate type. Moreover, conglomerate acquisitions accounted for more than $11 billion of the $12.6 billion in assets acquired through large acquisitions of manufacturing and mining firms during the same year."[10]

In addition to the regulatory changes and the propitious business environment, something of a bandwagon effect may also have contributed to the craze—but whatever the reasons, corporate leaders quickly became convinced of the effectiveness of conglomerates. (The exception was the University of Chicago view that risk diversification was more appropriately undertaken by investors rather than by companies.) As the *Journal of Business and Technology Law* study states, at the time "many of the leading executives believed that corporate diversification, through the acquisition of related and unrelated business, would establish a large corporation with increased efficiency and reduced potential risk." The idea was that "corporations could more easily and effectively manage a number of unrelated businesses through the use of the resources and administration of a single, large corporation"—and this would both mitigate risk and prompt synergistic growth. If a large corporation simultaneously had business operations in, say, energy, air travel, plastics, telecommunications, and electronics, then it would be in a safer position if any one of those sectors were to fall into a period of difficulty—conglomerates mitigated risk by diversifying into a wide variety of different sectors. Similarly, if they found success in one sector, they could use the proceeds to invest in other areas. Finally, these companies found that their diverse portfolio of businesses could boost the performance of their leadership talent, as well. New executives could be cycled through different lines of business, from which they would gain an invaluable and diverse set of skills that would ultimately redound the to the company's advantage.

One such conglomerate that rose to prominence in this era was the International Telephone & Telegraph Company (ITT), which was founded in 1920 in New York by brothers Sosthenes and Hernand Behn as a holding company for telephone and telegraph companies they owned in the Caribbean, including the Puerto Rico Telephone Company and the Cuban Telephone Company. From the beginning, the Behn brothers were ambitious about expanding their company through acquisitions and branching into new lines of business—and in

1925, the company broke into telephone manufacturing when it bought a subsidiary of AT&T responsible for building telephone equipment.

After World War II, the company continued expanding its telecommunications business throughout the Americas and elsewhere—and in 1959 Sosthenes Behn was succeeded as the company's leader by Harold Geneen, who had previously worked at the Raytheon Corporation. Geneen enthusiastically continued the company's record of expansion and pushed to diversify its business by taking on new and often unrelated areas. In its obituary for him upon his death in 1997, *The Economist* called Geneen the "emperor of acquisitions" and wrote that he "postulated that a company could successfully invest in any sort of business anywhere. The company imposed discipline on those units by setting strict financial targets; and kept on growing by acquiring new firms with its own highly-rated shares."[11] As the *New York Times* wrote in a retrospective, ITT under Geneen was "the very model of a multinational conglomerate" and "an incredible deal-making machine, acquiring a company a week at one point. ITT ended up owning 350 companies in 80 countries," including "hotels, insurance, rental cars, grass seed, frozen foods, bread and billboards."[12]

A company like ITT, with such a broad range of different lines of business under one corporate roof, may seem to resemble the ecosystem companies today that are creating powerful new value propositions by reaching across different sectors of the economy. Indeed, the conglomerates of the 1960s and 1970s (and earlier) prefigured today's ecosystems and share a few important commonalities with them: both grow by extending their offerings to meet customer needs and by expanding into new lines of business, sometimes through acquiring external companies, and sometimes by organically growing the business.

But at the same time, what's happening today is fundamentally different—in several important ways. First, in many cases, a conglomerate's component parts often did not fit together naturally; that is to say, they were not combined with the intention that they would work together harmoniously. Rather, they came together in most cases only because of the capital advantages of consolidation—or for other, somewhat ill-conceived reasons. Many conglomerates would take on entirely new businesses with very little customer overlap, or with few opportunities for creating synergies with their existing offerings. This was the so-called firm-as-portfolio model, in which a conglomerate's many divisions and acquisitions were seen as analogous to an investor's portfolio. A second important difference between conglomerates and ecosystems is their emphasis on collaboration—while conglomerates were content to do most things on their own, today's ecosystem players rely heavily on external, third-party companies or contractors to develop products and services on a common platform in the best interest of serving customer needs. And third, ecosystems tend to have business models that are quite different from those of conglomerates. While conglomerates generally relied on traditional business models, the most successful ecosystem players today favor a model of growing the pie in collaboration with other players and then sharing the value they have collectively created.

DISNEY'S HYBRID MODEL

One company that developed an especially forward-thinking model that both built on the conglomerate structure and prefigured today's ecosystem companies was Walt Disney Productions, now known as the Walt Disney Company. Brothers Walt and Roy O. Disney founded their studio in 1923, during a time when advances in filmmaking and animation were rapidly opening new creative possibilities. The studio soon found success with a series of short films that combined animation and live action—and thereafter made fast strides, developing its first sound film, *Steamboat Willie*, in 1928 and its first feature-length animated film, *Snow White and the Seven Dwarfs*, in 1937. *Snow White* proved a massive success—and with the proceeds, Disney began the process of buying a new 51-acre property in Burbank, California, where the company's studios are still headquartered today. The complex was finished by 1939, and the next year, the company made its initial public offering.

As the 1940s wore on, the Walt Disney studios grew more organized and efficient, pumping out numerous successful animated features, including *Pinocchio*, *Dumbo*, and *Bambi*. After the US entered World War II, the studio faced production challenges as many of the studio's staff members were drafted, and declining box office numbers as audiences had less money and less time for leisure. Nevertheless, the studio pressed on, and after the war was able to diversify into live-action features and TV programs.[13]

This was around the time when it started to become apparent that Disney was destined to become more than just an exceptionally successful maker of films. In 1948, with the war still a recent memory, Walt Disney sent a memo to his studio production designer outlining preliminary plans for what he called Mickey Mouse Park, a small park that he initially proposed building on an eight-acre lot across the street from the Disney studios in Burbank. The idea, as Disney put it, was to preempt the disappointment of fans who "come to Hollywood and find there's nothing to see."[14] As his vision for the park grew, Disney soon decided that his dreams were bigger than the Burbank location would allow, and in 1953 he bought a tract of land in Anaheim, California. Construction began the following year and by 1955, the park, which by then he had named Disneyland, opened.

The new park was an instant hit, and quickly began attracting hordes of fans. But the idea represented more than just a thoughtful and creative leader working to fulfill the dreams of his young fans—it was also a brilliant instance of a company leveraging its existing strengths to break into new areas. Indeed, the park was indicative of Disney's vision for a multi-pronged strategic approach in which the company's different divisions and endeavors would feed into and build off of one another, ultimately adding up to more than the sum of their parts.

While Disney forged this model many decades before the technological developments that precipitated our current era of digital ecosystems, its many synergies and its spanning of industry lines bear a distinct resemblance to some of the most dominant ecosystem players today. And like today's ecosystem players, Disney was also intent on building a suite of products and experiences that would provide what their customers wanted and needed in many different areas: not only in TV and film, but in books, travel, toys, and music—they were, in other words, meeting customers' needs in a set of end-to-end customer journeys. We might ask ourselves: was Disney an ecosystem company—far, far ahead of the curve? While the company's far-sighted strategic thinking represented a move toward ecosystem strategy, it differed in several important ways. Perhaps most importantly, Disney opted to do and build most everything by itself; rather than participating in a community of interconnected external businesses, Disney for the most part chose to build the community on its own.

Ultimately, Disney's model was a crucial mid-step between conglomerates and ecosystem companies—a brief glimmer of the possibilities on the horizon. Through the rest of the twentieth century, Disney would continue to grow and thrive, building a number of other theme parks, most notably Walt Disney World in Florida, expanding its TV operation, and acquiring numerous other companies.

CONGLOMERATES ELSEWHERE

Outside of the US, conglomerates also became a popular form, for similar reasons but under slightly different circumstances. As an article in the *Harvard Business Review* explains, while these business groups "may be called different things in different countries—*qiye jituan* in China, *business houses* in India, *grupos económicos* in Latin America, *chaebol* in South Korea, and *holdings* in Turkey"—they are essentially the same kind of arrangement.[15]

In Japan there were the zaibatsu, or "wealth cliques," a type of conglomerate that arose in the late nineteenth century following the Meiji Restoration, as the Japanese government sought to encourage economic growth and speed up the country's industrialization. The business leaders who grew out of this effort soon assembled into a network of family-controlled empires, the four most prominent of which were Mitsui, Mitsubishi, Sumitomo, and Yasuda. The zaibatsu typically reached into a multitude of different sectors, including textiles, mining, foreign trade, and insurance, among many others. The zaibatsu also participated in war industries during the Russo-Japanese War in 1904 and 1905, and World War I, and were able to expand significantly during that time. After Japan was defeated in World War II, the allied powers sought to dismantle the zaibatsu, though in practice they were only partially successful in doing so. Before long, the remnants of the zaibatsu and the individual companies that had been part of them began forming into loosely organized alliances that functioned in many ways similarly to their large, centralized, family-controlled predecessors—and as such, the zaibatsu continued to play a large role in the modern economic development of Japan.[16]

In Korea, a group of conglomerates rose to prominence as they helped the South Korean government rebuild after the devastation of the Korean War, which lasted from 1950 to 1953. Many of the companies, in fact, had their origins in the period of the Japanese occupation of Korea up until the end of World War II, and drew inspiration from the Japanese zaibatsu. During the reconstruction period following the Korean war, these companies, called chaebol, benefited greatly from the government's interest in speeding along the recovery and rebuilding vital industries like oil and steel. According to an article from the Council on Foreign Relations, "These enterprises flourished under the leadership of General Park Chung-hee, who led a military coup in 1961 and then served as president from 1963 to 1979. As part of Park's export-driven development strategy, his authoritarian government prioritized preferential loans to export businesses and insulated domestic industries from external competition."[17]

The word *chaebol* can be translated as "money faction" or "wealth clan," and as such, like the Japanese zaibatsu, the chaebol were almost entirely family-owned. According to a retrospective article on CNET, another defining feature of the chaebol is that they, like American conglomerates, span multiple sectors: "Not only must a conglomerate be family-owned to be considered a true chaebol, the conglomerate must have businesses in at least two disparate areas. . . . For example, Samsung Group, South Korea's largest chaebol, is known for its flagship subsidiary, Samsung Electronics . . . but it also owns subsidiaries that run a luxury hotel, build crude oil tankers and sell life insurance."

As the twentieth century wore on, the chaebol continued to move into new sectors and export their products into foreign markets, consolidating their power and strengthening South Korea's economy. As the Council on Foreign Relations article explains, "Exports grew from just 4 percent of [South Korea's] GDP in 1961 to more than 40 percent by 2016, one of the highest rates globally. Over roughly the same period, the average income of South Koreans rose from $120 per year to more than $27,000 in today's dollars. As South Korea lifted millions out of poverty, the parallel rise of chaebol embedded the conglomerates into the narrative of South Korea's postwar rejuvenation."

While they arose out of different political and economic circumstances—and often in direct response to certain regulatory changes, or government programs, or even wars—the different varieties of conglomerates around the world were generally part of a wave that continued to grow and grow throughout the twentieth century. As one business commentator wrote in the *New York Times*, "The different enterprises of the Japanese zaibatsu, the Korean chaebol and Turkish and Indian groups . . . have profited by working together both formally and informally. The gains of staying close are often especially large in developing economies, where credit, trust, expertise and good government relations are all very costly, if they can be purchased at all."[18]

But there were problems around the corner for conglomerates—at least in the West.

THE EVOLUTION OF CONGLOMERATES IN THE WEST

The model of the sector-spanning conglomerate might have made sense during its heyday in the mid-twentieth century. But by the 1980s, a confluence of trends was putting the conglomerate model under increasing pressure. Global markets were becoming far more efficient, especially with investors diversifying their portfolios of investments. The same was true for talent—as access to talent became easier globally, the market for talent became much more transparent and efficient. At the same time, some of the disadvantages of large conglomerates became more apparent: it turned out that managing a multitude of different divisions with different needs, goals, and motivations brought operational and organizational challenges that were extremely difficult to tackle under a broad conglomerate structure. Very often, being bigger and more complex meant tolerating more and more inefficiency.

For example, as we mentioned earlier, some conglomerates felt that owning a diverse array of businesses would help them to train leadership talent by enabling them to draw on resources from across all of their divisions. With such an advantage, these conglomerates presumed, they would be able to use their superior talent to drive better execution and achieve better results. But, while this may have been true to some degree, the increasingly efficient overall market for talent largely muted any advantage. Similarly, many conglomerates were confident that by using funds generated from their cash-cow businesses, they could invest in other businesses to drive better returns—a confidence that was only bolstered by interest rate regimes of the past. But here too their advantage was undercut by the increasingly efficient financial markets. All of this together put many conglomerates in a tough position and forced many to shed the subsidiaries they'd acquired during the boom.[19]

As an analysis from the *Harvard Business Review* explains, "Conglomerates were all the rage in the United States and Europe for decades, but . . . by the early 1980s, they had been laid low by their poor performance, which led to the idea that focused enterprises were better at creating shareholder value than diversified companies were."[20]

Accelerating the trend, the incoming Reagan administration took a more relaxed approach to antitrust enforcement than previous administrations had, and under its tenure the Federal Trade Commission became much more amenable to corporate mergers and acquisitions.[21] Somewhat counterintuitively, this more relaxed approach only compounded the difficulties facing the large conglomerates that grew to prominence in the 1960s and 1970s since it helped create conditions for a wave of corporate takeovers. As an academic study of the period explains, this brought about a golden age of what were called "bust up" takeovers, in which "raiders bought conglomerates and financed the deal through the post-acquisition sale of their separated parts." As the decade continued and more and more conglomerates started to feel the effects of the environment shifting against them, this practice became commonplace. At the same time, "diversified firms not threatened by takeover voluntarily shed unrelated operations to focus on 'core businesses.'"[22]

As companies adjusted or suffered under such detrimental conditions, the consensus view of corporate executives and business analysts shifted rapidly against the conglomerate structure. Over time, this new consensus became more and more engrained, and soon, it was so widely accepted that stock markets began to operate under the assumption that conglomerates were worth less than the sum of their parts, and valued their stock accordingly—this became known as the conglomerate discount.[23] This made conglomerates, especially in the West, even less competitive, and they soon fell behind—especially in delivering shareholder returns. The fallout from this phenomenon was widely felt, and ultimately put pressure on companies of all sorts to clean up and focus on their own turf, rather than searching for new, unrelated sectors to invade.

By the end of the 1980s, the combined effect of these trends was unmistakable: conglomerates were on their way out. Looking back on the decade in 1991, *The Economist* called the conglomerate craze "almost certainly the biggest collective error ever made by American business."[24]

Curiously, while this held true in the West (with a handful of notable exceptions), the story was considerably different in other parts of the world, where conglomerates continued to grow. In countries like China, India, and Turkey, these organizations continued to prosper—and grew even more complex and diversified still—long after the conglomerate discount became conventional wisdom in the West. As the *Harvard Business Review* study previously cited explains, "Conglomerates may be regarded as dinosaurs in the developed world, but in emerging markets, diversified business groups continue to thrive . . . [and] are becoming increasingly diversified. On average, they set up a new company every 18 months, more than half the time in a sector unrelated to their existing operations. Most of them are profitable."[25]

Why is this? In countries like the US and the UK, as markets became more efficient over the course of the latter half of the twentieth century, and conglomerates faced more challenging conditions, many businesspeople came to feel that focused enterprises were inherently better than diversified, multi-sectoral conglomerates. But elsewhere, circumstances were not as stacked against the conglomerate model. In certain local contexts around the world—including economies that had still some inefficiencies in labor, capital, and other areas—the idea of bringing many different lines of business together under one corporate roof continued to be attractive. And in many cases, organizations have found ways to overcome the disadvantages that have hindered some conglomerates in developing economies in the past. According to the *Harvard Business Review* article, a "major factor in their effectiveness . . . is that their leaders have stopped relying on family members and associates to oversee companies and created a formal management layer, called the group center, which is organized around the office of the group chairperson. That mechanism is helping smart business groups spot more opportunities and capitalize on them while retaining their identity and values."[26]

When we look at all of the ways that sectors and industries have changed and evolved over these many decades, what is perhaps most striking is that these developments unfolded relatively slowly (that is, compared to what's happening today), and in response to a variety of different drivers. These tectonic shifts in the marketplace happened over entire generations, as technologies improved, and consumer behaviors and expectations evolved, and as broader societal issues— like the need for sustainable energy, policy changes, and geopolitical developments—exerted pressure on businesses. Ultimately, while these changes were sweeping and transformative, companies for the most part had plenty of time to adapt and change their business models.

As we will see in the next chapter, the twenty-first century would bring with it a much, much faster pace of change, driven by new technological developments and consumer patterns. Suddenly, we began to see massive changes in the economy—the sort of changes that used to play out over multiple decades—happening in the space of just a few years.

2

The Walls Come Tumbling Down

The Dawn of an Ecosystem Economy

In 2007 and 2008, Apple and its then-CEO Steve Jobs were at a crossroads.

A decade earlier, in 1997, nearly twelve years after being forced out of the company he cofounded, Jobs had returned to Apple and was quickly placed at the company's helm. At the time of his return, the company was teetering on the edge of bankruptcy—Jobs knew that to save the company he would have to act quickly and decisively. The only way to survive, he concluded, was to cut out the company's many extraneous endeavors and focus all of its energies into a handful of core products that would rely on Apple's major strengths, especially design.

Apple's signature personal computers would certainly be one of these products, but Jobs could also see that personal computers were evolving—and that the internet would soon make it possible for all sorts of commerce and consumption to take place on computers. This was especially true, he could see, of music consumption. So Jobs put one of his strongest and most innovative teams on developing what would become the iPod, a small personal device for playing digital music.

The iPod, of course, became a huge hit as the digital music business soared and as Apple introduced iTunes to support it.[1] Soon, though, Jobs began thinking ahead to what would be next for the company, and by January 2007, he had unveiled the iPhone, a sleek personal device that would incorporate all the design refinements of Apple's previous devices as well as a sophisticated, new, all-touch interface.[2]

As tech enthusiasts lined up around the country to get one of the first iPhones, it started to become apparent just how powerful this device could be. It would make phone calls, send emails, manage a calendar, and browse the internet—all things that previous mobile devices like the BlackBerry had been able to do.[3] But Jobs and others at Apple could see that the iPhone had still more potential. What they didn't see, at least not immediately, was that the iPhone wouldn't be able to fully capitalize on that potential unless there was a robust infrastructure for building a wide variety of applications to expand the device's functionality. And in order for that to happen, outside developers would be needed—Apple by itself simply wouldn't be able to develop the hundreds of thousands of applications that would be needed to unleash the full power of the iPhone.

Initially, however, Jobs wanted to keep the third-party developers at arms-length, directing them to develop web-based applications that users would access through the iPhone's built-in Safari web browser. According to Walter Isaacson's biography of Jobs, the Apple CEO initially dismissed the possibility of third-party native applications for iPhone, "partly because he felt his team did not have the bandwidth to figure out all the complexities that would be involved in policing third-party app developers."[4]

Jobs and Apple soon relented, however, releasing a software developer kit and in July 2008 opening a new platform that they called the App Store. It was what *Wired* magazine would later call a "defining moment in the history of personal computing."[5] It not only made downloading mobile software (or applications) easy and simple, but placed Apple at the center of (and in charge of) a thriving marketplace where transformative new technological solutions would be built. Suddenly, Apple was no longer just a computer maker that had branched into mobile phones; it was the platform operator for a multitude of innovative software developers and other digital businesses.

This was the birth of the ecosystem that Apple would build around mobile devices in the coming years, though it would eventually enhance or build ecosystems centered on broad-based offerings as well. While the development was truly significant, it's important to remember that Apple was building on well-trodden ground in moving toward an app-based ecosystem. For many years already, Microsoft had been building its Windows platform as an ecosystem of sorts for PC-based applications, enlisting the help of third-party developers to make software to run alongside native Microsoft applications like Word and Internet Explorer. Indeed, Apple itself had in a similar fashion already built a kind of ecosystem around computer applications for its line of personal computers.

THE FOUR HURDLES

You might wonder why all of this began to unfold during this period specifically. If ecosystems are so great, why didn't they come sooner? As we saw in the previous chapter, by the time the ecosystem transformation had begun, the borders between different sectors of the economy had been around for a long time. In fact, there were several historical forces that had been actively keeping sectors discrete from one another—forces that made it difficult for businesses in one sector to move into another and form cross-sectoral value propositions. We might think of these forces as hurdles that stood in the way of companies hoping to work across multiple different sectors.

One hurdle was the problem of distribution. It used to be that businesses needed a physical presence, a tangible point of distribution, in order to reach customers. Retailers needed stores, banks needed branches, insurance companies needed networks of insurance agents. If you were a company looking to make a cross-sectoral play, you would inevitably come up against your lack of the distribution channels used by other businesses in that sector.

A second hurdle was the problem of data. In many sectors, businesses collected and maintained their own, unique, sector-specific data sets, which helped them to gain deep insights into their customers' needs and habits. An outside organization from a different sector that did not have access to such data, then, would be unable to compete against the insiders' data advantage. Banks and other financial institutions, for example, collected massive and sophisticated sets of data in order to assess lending risk. But without access to such data, any business from outside the financial sector that was considering a proposition involving banking would be unable to make financially prudent decisions about lending. Again, it was more trouble than it was worth for outsiders hoping to move in.

The third hurdle was the problem of systems. In the past, almost every sector had expensive and complex infrastructure backing it up—not just the aforementioned physical locations and the data capacity, but also sophisticated technological systems that supported its work: the machinery, computer systems, and other specialized equipment necessary to operate successfully. This, too, meant that companies already working within a particular sector enjoyed a distinct advantage over any outsider looking to move in.

The fourth and final hurdle was the problem of access to the supply chain. Newcomers to a sector would have found it difficult to compete with established players' access to, and familiarity with, key parts of the supply chain. While we have described these four hurdles as discrete from one another for the purposes of helping you to understand the forces in play, it is important to note that, in fact, these four hurdles are all interconnected and overlap with one another to some extent. In any case, the combined force of all four hurdles made it exceedingly difficult for a business in one industry to move into another; the established players in that industry had too many advantages of incumbency. Trying to diversify in a strategic way and form cross-sectoral value propositions to meet customer needs holistically was simply not feasible in most instances.

As technology grew more sophisticated and consumer preferences evolved, the information age took off in earnest, and before long consumers could wield what once would have been considered the power of a supercomputer in the palms of their hands. The combined force of these developments helped companies begin to overcome the four hurdles, creating the conditions in which ecosystems could thrive for the first time. This was an era that we might call Ecosystem 1.0. In the years ahead, these tech and consumer trends would drive down the cost of doing business, create huge opportunities for innovation, and begin to dissolve the borders between traditional sectors. If we want to fully understand how this came to pass, we will need to take a close look at each of the two changes that precipitated the shift: the rapid evolution of technology and the shift in consumer trends and behavior. First, let's consider technology.

THE GREAT ACCELERATION OF TECHNOLOGICAL PROGRESS

By the mid-2000s, the world had already become accustomed to a steady pace of technological innovation—stunning new technologies and new ways of using technology were emerging every year. By some measures, technology was improving exponentially. But with the rise of the internet and mobile devices, the world saw a sudden acceleration, as all sorts of communication and activity moved online: the game-changing innovations kept coming faster and faster.

This created some incredible opportunities for business, and soon enough we began to see companies like Amazon, eBay, and Microsoft reaping the rewards. At the same time, the transformational power of social media and social networking platforms started to become clear, as companies like Facebook, Twitter, and LinkedIn took off, connecting people not only to their friends, family, colleagues, and professional associates—but also to a wide array of news, entertainment, and information.

With the proliferation of the smartphone and mobile computing, the pace of innovation accelerated still more. Tech companies suddenly were able to make their products and services truly personalized, context-based, and accessible with just a quick tap. At the same time, the vast quantities of highly specific personal data that these new internet-connected devices collected, including location data, made it possible for companies to offer an ease of use that was fundamentally appealing to people on a psychological and emotional level. We as humans crave simplicity and instant gratification. And the advent of mobile and cloud computing meant that suddenly, we could get many of the things we wanted almost instantly, with the push of a button. The combined effect of all of this was that we started to see the lowering of the first hurdle previously discussed, as businesses began to solve the problem of distribution. Whereas in the past, companies looking to move into a new sector were faced with the daunting task of having to build out stores, branches, or other infrastructure, now advances in digital technology opened all sorts of new possibilities for reaching customers—including through smart phone apps. Before long, newcomers to any one particular sector found themselves on equal footing with established incumbents, at least in terms of the distribution problem to get access to customers. Today, while having a physical infrastructure like warehouses and fulfillment centers still gives some companies an advantage over others, it has also become much easier to connect with consumers because of developments in various modes of online technology.

As the twenty-first century has worn on, the pace of technological innovation has only continued to increase, driven by the easy availability of data, analytics capabilities, and computing power (see Figure 2.1). Significant improvements have become possible in a very short span of time. Simultaneously, the continued evolution of cheaper and more precise sensor technology has opened even more opportunities for companies to collect rich data sets. Meanwhile, augmented and virtual reality technologies (AR/VR) are emerging that will drastically reshape numerous areas of business and commerce as well as our daily lives. As we will see in the next chapter, these emerging technologies will create countless opportunities for new businesses and new services—like, for instance, digital twins, which are replicas of physical assets (like a car or a house) that enable users to customize, upgrade, repair, or alter their asset.[6]

As breakthroughs like this continue to emerge in new and unexpected ways, our technological capabilities will continue to develop more and more. What does this look like in action? For starters, it means a vast number of new, internet-connected devices coming online. Around 2018, the world hit a striking milestone: for the first time ever, the number of internet-connected devices in the world overtook the number of people.[7] And as technology becomes more sophisticated, gets better at solving our problems, and as people get more comfortable letting technology solve their problems, the number of devices in circulation continues to shoot up at a head-spinning rate. In the decade between 2010 and 2020, the number of internet-connected devices in the world more than doubled.[8]

There are differing estimates as to where the numbers will go in the future, but depending on whom you ask, the number of connected devices may be five to ten times the global population by the end of the 2020s.[9] And these devices will become more and more embedded in people's lives. Soon, the average person in the developed world will live enmeshed in a web of hundreds, or perhaps thousands, of connected devices that support and guide their lives. It is not inconceivable that this number will continue to increase by orders of magnitude, especially when we take into consideration new and emerging modes of transportation as well as the rise of digital personal health care—both of which will involve even more devices, which may in some cases even be embedded in our bodies.

FIGURE 2.1   **How technology development accelerated economic development over the last two centuries**

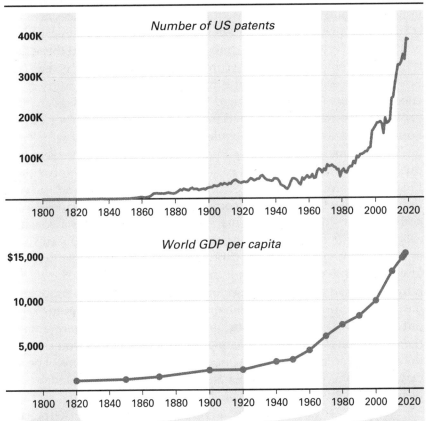

Number of US patents

World GDP per capita

Late 18th century	*Early 20th century*	*1960s and 1970s*	*Today and tomorrow*
1st Industrial Revolution	**2nd Industrial Revolution**	**3rd Industrial Revolution**	**4th Industrial Revolution**
Steam and hydro power, mechanical production, weaving loom	Electricity, mass production, division of labor	Electronics, computers and IT, early automated production	Connectivity, intelligence, flexible automation, tech embedded in the physical world

Note: Number of patents is a decent indicator of innovation, but is by no means a perfect measure.

Sources: Maddison Project database, real GDP per capita in 2011 U.S. dollars; U.S. Patent and Trademark Office; McKinsey Global Institute analysis.'

The consequences of this proliferation are numerous, and it can be difficult to wrap our heads around them. But one of the most important—and tangible—consequences is that these devices are generating vast quantities of data. Every internet-connected smartphone, watch, refrigerator, car, and thermostat generates data. And those data can be incredibly useful, giving companies deep insights into customer's preferences, habits, and priorities. According to one study referenced in *Forbes*, between 2010 and 2020 "the amount of data created, captured, copied, and consumed in the world increased from 1.2 trillion gigabytes to 59 trillion gigabytes, an almost 5,000% growth."[10]

At the same time, as greater and greater volumes of data were produced, it became cheaper and easier to store and process those data. Meanwhile, breakthroughs in Artificial Intelligence (AI) and the continued exponential growth of computing power gave businesses the ability to transform disparate pieces of information about a consumer's immediate desires and behavior into insights about the consumer's broader needs. These incredibly deep insights, combined with the low cost and easy availability of the data, began to lower the second hurdle that had been keeping sectors separate, solving the problem of data. This, in turn, made it easier and cheaper for companies to branch out and pursue all sorts of opportunities. If you're a tech company, and the data gleaned from your existing products are giving you a highly detailed and accurate sense of your customers' needs in terms of health care or banking, that would open up valuable opportunities for you to design and deliver propositions in the health care or banking sectors.

At the same time, these new advances in technology also lowered the third hurdle, helping to solve the problem of systems. In the past, incumbents in a sector would derive a huge advantage over outsiders from their specialized, proprietary systems and equipment. But now, with the advent of cloud-based infrastructure and as-a-service business models, these system capabilities are becoming increasingly modular and scalable. Together with the digitalization of non-IT systems, this is making the third hurdle much less of a problem for new entrants to a particular sector. At the same time, the evolution of technology, including the availability of data and cloud-based capabilities powered by global online connectivity, also aided significantly in helping new entrants find capabilities they might need from various parts of the supply chain. The wealth of information available online including through online networks (both personal and business-oriented) made it much easier to get access to suppliers and to get information on their performance history and background. All of this contributed to significantly lowering the fourth hurdle.

With all four hurdles lowered either partially or completely, businesses of all stripes were given the opportunity to begin experimenting with cross-sectoral value propositions.

CONSUMER BEHAVIOR EVOLUTION

While technology has grown by leaps and bounds, and perhaps in part *because* of this growth, consumer behaviors and expectations changed as well. This is the other major piece of what precipitated the emergence of Ecosystem 1.0. As technology made everyday activities and business interactions easier, quicker, and more personalized, we as consumers became more and more demanding in our expectations. Consumers increasingly valued businesses that were able to predict what they wanted and deliver it to them instantly—or as close to instantly as possible. As Steve Jobs famously observed, "A lot of times, people don't know what they want until you show it to them."[11]

These changing consumer habits are perhaps most apparent when we consider the generations that grew up with some or all of the technologies that precipitated these habits: Millennials and Gen Z. And their changing habits and expectations extend beyond just impatience. They are much more likely than older demographics to be influenced by mobile apps, to follow brands online, and to make purchasing decisions based on social media. The trends are even more accentuated among the youngest—for instance, a large subsection of the Gen Z cohort, 40 percent, say that social media is the most important factor influencing their purchasing decisions.[12]

While younger people may offer a starker picture of these trends—and a good sense of what to expect in the future—the changes in consumer expectations and behaviors are universal and only accelerating over time. Consumers of all ages have increasingly become much more comfortable getting their services from providers that span traditional sectors of the economy—for example, getting financial services like a credit card from Apple or an insurance policy from an app-based provider instead of from a traditional company.

Why is this? As it turns out, the speed and convenience that consumers experience in one sector influences their expectations about what companies should be able to do for them in other sectors. And in turn, certain industries, namely, the tech industry, are setting the standards for other more traditional industries in terms of speed, functionality, and ease of use. One effect of this has been a proliferation of lightning-fast shipping options from online retailers—and those retailers and providers who can't keep up are falling behind.

This, of course, breeds more impatience, and contributes to a self-perpetuating cycle that carries over into other sectors. Think, for instance, of a person who has become accustomed to booking a house cleaner with a single tap on their smartphone, or ordering paper towels by voice through a smart speaker and having them delivered the same day by Amazon. Even though banking is a completely different sector, the speed and efficiency with which a consumer can order paper towels is still going to make that person less willing to wait in line at a bank to sign up for a checking account—and therefore more likely to bank through an app-based provider. All of this together has helped to create a customer base that increasingly wants companies to predict what customers want, when they want it, and to present it through their preferred means of delivery (often a smartphone app).

This is just as true in other countries as it is in the US—in fact, as we'll explore later, the trend may be even more pronounced in China. Huge numbers of people in China have become accustomed to the convenience of the smartphone era. Imagine, for example, a person who is used to instantly ordering food through a mobile app. Even though health care is a completely unrelated industry, this person will, in all likelihood, be less patient navigating the process of getting a medical procedure done through traditional channels. In turn, they will be much more likely to try an app like Good Doctor, a platform operated by the Ping An insurance company that allows patients to make online bookings with doctors and connect through the app to receive diagnoses, advice, and treatments. Communications that used to unfold over multiple appointments, taking days or even weeks, can now be resolved almost instantaneously through a comprehensive app with a simple, easy-to-use interface.

But it's not just about impatience. As Apple has introduced sleek and intuitive new product designs like the iPhone's multi-touch interface, consumers begin to expect that same quality of design and ease of use in other areas of their lives, too—in their kitchen appliances, in their washing machines, even in their cars. One of the ways that Tesla, the electric carmaker, was able to become so successful, was by being the first to replicate in a car the same kind of easy-to-use interfaces that consumers have come to expect from tech products.

Customers both young and old also value being able to get all the services they need in one place, and they are willing to change providers to get the sort of seamless experience they want. An overwhelming majority of consumers today are willing to switch brands in order to get a consistent experience, with multiple needs met by the same provider. This preference may be driven in part by customers' increasing intolerance of anything less than the utmost simplicity and convenience when it comes to transactions on mobile devices: recent studies have shown that roughly nine in ten customers will abandon items saved in their online shopping carts if the checkout and payment process is too complicated. Overall, we have seen consumers become more and more open to embracing change and trying new ways of getting goods and services, especially if doing so creates a more streamlined, simple, all-in-one customer experience.

Finally, in addition to the technological developments and consumer changes, there are a few other wild-card factors that have shaped the emergence of ecosystems and will continue to shape their development in the future. As the need to address climate change has become a global priority, new ecosystems have sprung up around sustainability, in areas such as clean energy and electric cars—and these will continue to evolve as governments get more and more serious about tackling the problem. Geopolitical developments around the world will also shape ecosystems, as more internationalist and more nationalist factions push for incentives that will, respectively, either make ecosystems more globally oriented or make them more regionally oriented. And a host of policy questions, both in the US and elsewhere, ranging from data privacy to antitrust to topics of wealth accumulation and wealth concentration, will have the potential to either propel or impede the growth of ecosystems. (We will cover each of these questions in more detail in the next chapter.)

ECOSYSTEM 1.0

As technology and consumers both continued to change, and as the other, more minor factors continued to exert influence, these trends started to build off of one another, and before long they had triggered a major shift in the way companies do business. The world had finally reached a point of critical mass at which the ecosystem model became feasible for a broad range of players, triggering a massive reshuffling of the economy.

By offering products, services, and propositions that were difficult for individual companies to create on their own, ecosystems drew in more and more customers, who produced even more data—and as better ways of analyzing those data emerged, it became easier and easier to fashion even better offerings, which in turn helped attract more customers. Along the way, customers' costs went down significantly, even as they got more and more value out of the arrangement.

All of this together had the effect of lowering the hurdles that had traditionally kept sectors apart even more. As this played out, consumers quickly adapted, becoming much more intolerant of inconvenience and more likely to switch products or services. As the process continued, an opportunity soon opened up for a new type of cross-sectoral business, unlike the old conglomerate model—one driven not by the marginal capital efficiencies of merging diverse lines of business under one roof, or by the talent-scale benefits of doing so, but by a singular focus on delivering value for the customer.

Back in the 1960s and 1970s heyday of conglomerates, customers usually didn't derive much of a benefit from companies owning massive and varied business interests. It didn't do customers any good for ITT, the telecommunications giant, to also own a chain of hotels, or the company that made Wonder Bread, Continental Baking.[13] What advantage is there to getting your bread and your phone service from the same company? But for the new companies rising to prominence during the era of the internet and cloud computing, the move to a cross-sectoral frame would be driven by a genuine passion for adding customer value.

Breaking down the barriers between industries gave companies a way of serving customers as they had always wanted to be served: with everything all together, all at once. Customers had always been attracted to the idea of getting as many things as possible from the same place—but only when it truly made sense. Just look at the rise of supermarkets, or later the rise of huge, big-box, one-stop shopping centers like Walmart, or even later the rise of all-in-one online retailers like Amazon. Again, the different sectors into which the economy had been organized for so long simply didn't make intuitive sense to most consumers. No consumer has ever felt a deep desire for a mortgage—what consumers want is a home, and acquiring a home involves a great deal beyond just a mortgage, including products and services that come from multiple different industries. As the barriers between industries continued to fade, and companies set about creating sector-spanning all-in-one platforms, they found they were finally able to fulfill customer needs on a holistic level, by giving them whole categories of services together, all at once. They became providers of homes, not mortgages. Of mobility, not cars. Of entertainment, not TV.

While this was a time of exciting possibility for many businesses, it was also a time of peril. For as these changes were taking place and companies were exploring their newfound powers, they also found themselves butting up against other players, often in unexpected ways. Suddenly, businesses had to compete, not just with their traditional competitors, but with all sorts of other businesses as well. Attacks could come from any direction—and there were bound to be fierce, unexpected encounters as businesses aggressively encroached on one another's territory. Many of the traditional protections that established companies enjoyed in the past were disappearing. The hurdles that had previously insulated them from outside attacks were either partially or completely lowered. No longer could incumbents take comfort in the advantage of having a powerful distribution infrastructure set up and in place, or a sophisticated set of data already assembled, or established technological systems, or access to critical parts of the supply chain.

ECOSYSTEMS ELSEWHERE

As is the case with any large-scale, far-reaching economic change, the way this shift played out wasn't uniform. In fact, it varied considerably between different parts of the world. Many of the visionaries emerged in Silicon Valley, of course—this was where Apple, Google, and others honed their ecosystem approach. But there has also been a great deal of ecosystem action in other parts of the world, particularly in the developing world and in the East, where in many cases, a unique set of circumstances helped drive the growth—including a strong concentration of young people and less of a history of robust, legacy industries. The combined effect of these conditions made ecosystem growth in these places especially explosive, and had a large impact on society that was immediately felt.

There have been three general patterns in the way that Ecosystem 1.0 emerged: the Chinese model, the model of other developing economies, and the model of the US and other Western countries. To get a fuller picture of how ecosystems emerged and developed around the world, let us explore each of these trajectories, beginning with China, where a unique convergence of factors made the emergence of Ecosystem 1.0 significantly faster and more explosive than in other parts of the world.

The massive Chinese internal market was special for many reasons. Perhaps most importantly, China's position as a hybrid socialist–market economy made it an especially conducive environment for ecosystem growth. First, the government took a keen interest in growing the tech sector and was willing to put considerable state resources behind that goal. Then there was the regulatory environment—the government's censorship of the internet, sometimes called the Great Firewall of China,[14] was extremely effective at preventing Western tech companies from capturing the Chinese market. At the same time, the regulatory laws around data and privacy were—especially in comparison to other markets, like the EU—different in ways that gave Chinese tech companies a leg up. There was also an enormous cohort of young, tech-savvy consumers newly accumulating wealth—and they were an ideal target audience for ecosystem offerings. In the US and so many other countries, it is the older generations who hold all the wealth while the young have little; but comparatively, China's younger generations have an unusually large share of that country's wealth. Finally, there was an overall curiosity and interest from Chinese customers about the promise of incorporating technology-enabled solutions in their everyday life. These special circumstances quickly created a new group of innovative giants with bold visions to capture customers into their own ecosystems.

First and foremost, there is Tencent. Today one of the world's largest tech companies, the Chinese firm started in 1998 and was at first focused on a PC-based instant messaging service known as QQ, though it soon began branching out, entering the online game market in 2003 and starting a Facebook-like social networking service called QZone in 2005. Like US tech companies' decision to allow third-party developers to build apps for their devices and software platforms, Tencent decided to allow third-party apps on Qzone, which helped fuel its growth and made it by 2010 the largest social media platform in China, with 492 million active users at the time.[15] This ultimately became the driving force of Tencent's ecosystem approach, allowing it to orchestrate a vast array of third-party companies. But this didn't happen overnight.

Back in 2011, as the smartphone space came to dominate the tech sector, Tencent launched its mobile messaging app WeChat. According to a *Business Insider* profile, although it started as a simple, WhatsApp-like service, "it grew explosively as it expanded into a kind of super-app that takes the place of Uber, GrubHub, Venmo, Craigslist, and a whole bunch of other services."[16] This super-app structure began in 2017, when WeChat launched its Mini Program or Mini-app feature, which allows developers to build pre-approved lightweight apps that are embedded within WeChat and function as an extension of it. The mini-apps proved incredibly popular as they allowed customers to use external services with just four clicks and without leaving WeChat or downloading a new app.

This development turned out to be pivotal, and was part of a concerted strategy to establish WeChat as a platform through openness to third parties.[17] It essentially changed WeChat—and by extension Tencent—from an app to more of a platform around which an ecosystem could be built. Before long, WeChat was at the center of a dynamic and vibrant new ecosystem. By the end of the 2010s, WeChat was clearly the largest Chinese super app, far ahead of its nearest rival, Alibaba's Alipay, and more popular on a daily basis.[18] There were more that 2.3 million WeChat mini-apps, although just a handful were widely used. Overall, WeChat became so deeply enmeshed in its customers' everyday experiences that *Fortune* called it, "effectively the operating system for people's digital lives in China."[19]

But Tencent's ecosystem strategy extends beyond just the super-app structure of WeChat. Apart from its social network arms QQ, Qzone, and WeChat, Tencent operates in a wide variety of different, often overlapping, sectors, including online advertising, digital media, gaming, and cloud.

Because of the synergies of its multifaceted approach, Tencent came to dominate in almost all of these categories—a stark difference from the landscape in the US, where the market is more fragmented among different players. In the US, for instance, at least as of this writing, a different company leads almost every sub-category within digital media. In other words, the company with the number one social network is different from the leader in video streaming, which is different from the leader in music streaming, online gaming, etc. In China,

Tencent sits atop the pack in every one of these categories. Ultimately, its success was a direct outcome of its decision to draw on the strength of its most popular offering, WeChat, and to build around it a powerful ecosystem centered on fulfilling all of the needs a customer might have.

Another prominent example of the explosive ecosystem growth in China is Alibaba, the e-commerce company started in 1999 by Jack Ma in the southeastern Chinese city of Hangzhou.[20]

After some initial difficulty obtaining funding, Alibaba began to grow quickly, seeking to leverage the power of small and medium-size offline businesses in China, and embarking on a campaign to convince Chinese consumers and companies to start using the internet. One of its biggest breaks arose out of its battle in the mid-2000s with the American company eBay, which was trying to expand into the Chinese market by buying a consumer-to-consumer (C2C) e-commerce website called Each.net. Ebay was determined to make the expansion work, and pumped resources into Each.net until it controlled 85 percent of the C2C e-commerce market in China. In response, Alibaba put its focus into developing and building its own C2C website, Taobao, investing a considerable sum into the site and announcing that it would let users sell their goods for free for three years. Alibaba and its Taobao site quickly made inroads with China's younger generations, and in 2005, the American internet giant Yahoo bought a $1 billion stake in the Chinese company.[21]

From there, Alibaba continued its ascent, making a big splash when it went public in the US in 2014 with what was, at the time, the biggest IPO in history. By the end of the 2010s, it had exceeded even Walmart in terms of sales and became one of the world's top 10 companies in terms of market cap.[22] At every point along the way, Alibaba was intent on building value from collaboration with other businesses and players rather than doing everything itself. According to a study of the company in the *Harvard Business Review*, Alibaba went about this, by "adopting a more open data architecture." This was a strategy, the article explained, that was "fundamentally different from the Western approach," which it said is characterized by a more cautious, guarded stance on issues of data.[23]

This focus on partnerships and ecosystems became central to Alibaba's ethos and integral to its explosive success. In 2004, around the time of the fight with eBay, Alibaba launched its online payments service, Alipay.[24] As the era of the smartphone took off, Alipay morphed into a mobile payments service, allowing users to send payments using QR codes. In 2018, Alipay rolled out subordinate mini-apps similar to those used by Tencent's WeChat, with everything from food delivery, to telehealth medical services, to digital entertainment, to e-commerce, in the form of Taobao. Though Alipay's mini-app ecosystem remained a step behind WeChat's, with between 1 and 2 million mini-apps by the end of the 2010s,[25] the company is still one of the world's largest e-commerce companies and as of 2021 ranked in the top ten companies worldwide in terms of market cap. As Ming Zeng, the former chief-of-staff and policy advisor to Jack Ma, proclaimed in the *Harvard Business Review*:

> Alibaba's special innovation, we realized, was that we were truly building an ecosystem: a community of organisms (businesses and consumers of many types) interacting with one another and the environment (the online platform and the larger off-line physical elements). Our strategic imperative was to make sure that the platform provided all the resources, or access to the resources, that an online business would need to succeed, and hence supported the evolution of the ecosystem.[26]

In other parts of the developing world, ecosystem growth started with a delay, but by the end of the 2010s started moving just as fast as in China. In these places, while there were not the same conditions that led to the early and explosive growth in China, there was still an environment conducive to rapid mass adoption of new technologies. These emerging markets, including countries like India, Brazil, Turkey, and increasingly, many African countries, tend to have big internal markets ideally suited to sustaining super apps and other similar propositions.

ECOSYSTEMS IN THE US

Then, of course, there are the American companies. In the US, as we previously noted, it was the tech companies that were quickest to embrace ecosystems because these were the companies that had the most experience adapting their business models to meet emerging needs and changing circumstances. They also enjoyed a head start on their competitors in other sectors when it came to leveraging data and mobile technologies— and had a history of establishing, fostering and sustaining software developer and app-based ecosystems. And even though these companies are now well-known, their advantage doesn't seem to be waning, and markets have remained enthusiastic about them: by the early 2020s, most of the companies with the world's highest market capitalizations were tech companies with robust digital ecosystems.

Take Amazon. The company started, of course, in the 1990s as an online retailer for books and other goods, and achieved early success during the dot-com boom by building an ecosystem of merchants, allowing third-party vendors to sell via their online platform and taking a cut. From there, Amazon began branching out, making a series of ecosystem plays in other areas, and building an array of sub-ecosystems that would fit within and support its broader framework.

In the mid-2000s, for example, the company started laying the groundwork for what would eventually become a major part of its business, the cloud computing subsidiary, Amazon Web Services (AWS). As *TechCrunch* explains, AWS began as an ecosystem play called Merchant.com, which was originally conceived "as a side business for Amazon.com" that could make money by extending Amazon's platform to other websites and helping third-party merchants to set up their own retail sites based on Amazon's e-commerce framework. As time wore on, Amazon officials began to see the potential of what they were building, and Merchant.com morphed into Amazon Web Services, a cloud computing service that provides servers, storage, networking, and security for startups and big companies alike, as well as the ability to build applications. According to the *TechCrunch* article, Amazon officials "started to think of this set of services as an operating system of sorts for the internet." Accordingly, they began to place greater emphasis on the endeavor and put more resources into growing it.[27] AWS soon became the leading cloud computing platform and began bringing in massive revenues—and before long, it had become a sub-ecosystem within Amazon's larger entity, focused on serving end-to-end business needs.

The rise of AWS and other cloud computing providers, in turn, helped to drive still more innovation, lowering the cost of computing power and fueling the conditions that drove the emergence of Ecosystem 1.0 in the first place. Startups, suddenly, could get the IT services they needed at a variable rather than a fixed cost—what Amazon called "pay as you go."[28] This created opportunities for new players, but it also made it much easier for established companies to enter new sectors, especially digital ones, and compete in unexpected ways.

This unexpected competition could happen in the other direction, too, with tech companies using the advantages of their data-supported platforms to break into traditional sectors. As Amazon grew, it began launching additional sub-ecosystems. One of the most prominent was focused on entertainment. In 2010, the company launched its television and film production subsidiary, Amazon Studios, focusing on creating original content to serve to customers via its streaming service, Amazon Prime Video. The company eventually even bought the iconic Hollywood studio Metro-Goldwyn-Mayer for $8.45 billion.[29] But the move into movies and TV was more than just a stab in the dark—it was part of the company's broader strategy to fulfill customers' needs and desires in multiple areas, and to grow as a result of that synergy. While Amazon's move may in some ways appear to fit more easily into the conglomerate model than an ecosystem model, in fact, the expansion leverages and builds upon much deeper synergies (see Figure 2.2). By creating its own video content, Amazon boosted its streaming service, Amazon Prime Video, which connects the work of other studios and creators, and ultimately delivers integrated digital entertainment value for the consumer beyond what their competitors are able to offer.

In the mid- and late-2010s, Amazon continued its expansion into non-tech sectors when it decided to expand into bricks-and-mortar retailing, building another sub-ecosystem focused on fulfilling customers' retail needs in the immediate, physical world. In 2015, it launched what would become a line of physical bookstores, Amazon Books (though it later shut down that venture),[30] and then in 2017, it acquired the grocery chain Whole Foods.[31] The following year, in 2018, the company began rolling out its chain of semi-automated convenience stores, Amazon Go, and several years later, announced a bricks-and-mortar apparel store, Amazon Styles. As the *New York Times* wrote, Amazon's efforts to move into physical retail markets "reflect a growing recognition by the company that certain categories of shopping are unlikely to move completely online."[32]

But tech companies are not the only American companies to see the benefit—or the necessity—of expanding across sector borders and building ecosystems. Lego, for instance, has moved beyond being just a maker of traditional toys (its classic plastic bricks) to focus on developing an ecosystem centered on play and entertainment. This ecosystem has grown to encompass an array of digital and non-digital offerings, including apps, online games, movies, books, and theme parks. And Tesla, the carmaker, has built an ecosystem focused on

FIGURE 2.2   **Overview of the Amazon Universe**

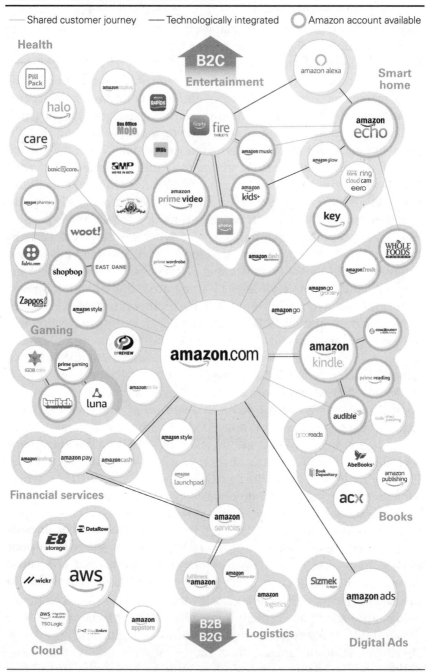

sustainable energy by branching into making home batteries and solar panels, in addition to their electric vehicles (EVs). With the full suite of Tesla products, customers can generate their own energy, store it in their houses, and use it to power their electric cars. To reflect the shift, the company changed its name from Tesla Motors to simply, Tesla, Inc.[33]

LOOKING BACK

The leaders of companies today can see what is happening. If they are not already pursuing ecosystem-based approaches and strategies, they are starting to think seriously about how they might—and about the existential threats that may be lurking across the boundaries of traditional sectors of the economy. Increasingly, more and more CEOs are worrying that companies in other industries might be able to use new technologies to learn more about their customers than they know themselves. But business leaders are not the only ones paying attention to the power of ecosystems. We can also see the transformative power they've had reflected in the attention they've received from governments. Regulators from India to Europe are paying close attention to the emergence and the success of ecosystems—especially with regard to profit concentration.

At the end of the day, this much is clear: companies that build, foster, and sustain ecosystems are not anomalous. They are not curiosities that can be dismissed as products of special circumstances—rather, they are at the center, or, more accurately, the top of the economy today. They are not outliers, but harbingers of the economy's future. And they are here to stay.

None of this is to say that ecosystem-based companies are foolproof or that they cannot fail. Many ecosystem-based companies have encountered difficulty, and there are plenty of examples of ecosystem failures. Like every other type of business, ecosystem-based businesses sometimes run up against unexpected obstacles, or suffer from poor planning and execution. There are several factors that can cause failure—these include being outcompeted by rivals who are able to find alternative, simpler, or more cohesive ways to deliver value; losing out to competitors with innovative value propositions; and finally, being unable to truly foster, develop, and grow the ecosystem once it's set up. Some examples of failed or troubled ecosystem businesses include Sony's Betamax videotape ecosystem of the 1980s, Nokia's

Symbian smart phone OS ecosystem of the 1990s and 2000s, the ride-sharing company Uber's ecosystem in China, and the social networking platform MySpace's ecosystem. In other words, working to build an ecosystem-oriented business is far from a guarantee of success.

But while they are not a panacea, ecosystems are closely correlated with stronger results. And the business world is taking notice. To understand just how much ecosystems dominate today, and how much of an outsized role they are playing in shaping the economy, we need only to take a look at a list of the largest companies in terms of market capitalization, as we did in this book's introduction. A significant majority of the top ten companies today are tech companies with robust ecosystem businesses (see Figure 2.3).

This list represents a stunning shift over the last twenty years. Even just ten years ago, the list looked very different. Apple and Microsoft were already there, but a large portion of the other companies were fossil fuel companies. Ten years before that, the list was more diverse: banks, insurance companies, drug companies, and old-style sector-spanning conglomerates.

Do these dynamics portend a sea change for every company? Of course not. People will still visit physical stores, heavy industry (with the benefit of technological advances, to be sure) will go on extracting and processing the materials essential to our daily lives, and countless other enterprises beyond the digital space will continue to channel the ingenuity of their founders and employees to serve a world of incredibly varied preferences and needs. It's obvious that ecosystems will not—and cannot—change everything.

But it's just as apparent that the effects of ecosystems on the competitive landscape have already been profound. As boundaries between industry sectors continue to blur, CEOs—many of whose companies have long commanded large revenue pools within traditional industry lines—will face off against companies and industries they never previously viewed as competitors. This new environment will play out by new rules and require different capabilities.

The stakes are only getting higher. As much as ecosystems have changed the world already, they will change still more in the future. But before we delve into the specifics of how to navigate that future, it's worth considering what that future will look like.

FIGURE 2.3 **Evolution of the list of world's largest market cap companies in the past two decades**

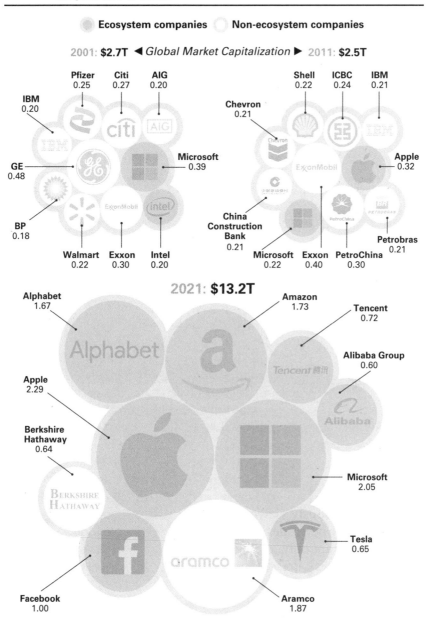

● Ecosystem companies   ○ Non-ecosystem companies

2001: **$2.7T** ◀ *Global Market Capitalization* ▶ 2011: **$2.5T**

| Pfizer 0.25 | Citi 0.27 | AIG 0.20 | | Shell 0.22 | ICBC 0.24 | IBM 0.21 |

IBM 0.20

Chevron 0.21

GE 0.48 — Microsoft 0.39 — Apple 0.32

BP 0.18

China Construction Bank 0.21

Walmart 0.22   Exxon 0.30   Intel 0.20

Microsoft 0.22   Exxon 0.40   PetroChina 0.30   Petrobras 0.21

2021: **$13.2T**

Alphabet 1.67

Amazon 1.73

Tencent 0.72

Alibaba Group 0.60

Apple 2.29

Berkshire Hathaway 0.64

Microsoft 2.05

Tesla 0.65

Facebook 1.00

Aramco 1.87

Source: S&P Capital IQ.

3

The Exhilarating Path Ahead

How the Uncertain Future Will Shape the Evolution of Ecosystems

Imagine an ordinary day several decades from now. You wake up to the sound of birds chirping and slowly ease into the morning, looking around the dark room. You saunter into the bathroom to relieve yourself. As you go to wash your hands, though, your smart home sends an alert to your bathroom mirror: the toilet automatically tested your urine and determined that your sodium levels are still too high. This has been going on for more than a week now. Last week, when the sensors in your toilet first noticed the increase, the artificial intelligence (AI) program that manages your grocery-delivery service automatically edited your order for the week, substituting low-sodium alternatives. Meanwhile, the cluster of devices that measure and record your vital signs—from a watch that measures your heart rate and temperature to a tiny subdermal sensor in your arm that studies your blood—have been busily analyzing your readings, trying to get to the bottom of the problem. Your health system has also been consulting your genome to determine if a genetic predisposition may be a contributing factor. Nevertheless, the answer remains elusive. The sodium problem is not going away. This time, the smart home display suggests booking a telehealth appointment with your doctor to discuss the issue, and pulls up available times.

As you walk into the next room to enjoy your low-sodium breakfast, another alert chimes on your phone: the big storm that forecasters have been talking about for the last few days is projected to sweep through your area tonight. As you sip your coffee, the morning news plays in the background and the display takes you through the preparations for the storm: with high wind gusts predicted, there is a decent chance that the power grid will be disrupted, so the house begins conserving energy and charging its reserve battery system to full capacity.

Next, your smart home system pulls up a virtual 3D model of your house and scans the entire structure for any weaknesses or vulnerabilities that could be a problem during the storm. This 3D model is part of a sophisticated, online augmented-reality tool that connects to the metaverse, an AR/VR platform that duplicates in virtual space objects from the physical world. The 3D virtual model, also known as a digital twin, allows for the remote inspection, troubleshooting, and evaluation of everything in your home from appliances and hardware to your house itself. And this is exactly what your smart home system begins to do now as it scans your house's roofing, siding, windows, and gutters for any potential problems.

Before the scan is finished, though, your phone chimes again to tell you it's time to go to work, so you step outside to find the self-driving car you ordered waiting in the driveway. The news program that you'd been watching inside, with the latest details on the storm, automatically transfers from your home TV to the car's screen and continues playing as you take out your computer and begin catching up on email, as relaxed as if the car were an extension of your own living room. As you gaze out the window, the early morning light reflects from the windows of nearby buildings and falls gently on the trees lining the street. The storm may be coming in a matter of hours, but for the time being it's a beautiful day. You decide to walk the last few blocks to work and with a simple voice command, the automated car pulls over to let you out before speeding on to its next pickup. The news program transfers seamlessly from the car's screen to your phone's, but you've already got the information you need, so you switch it off.

As you stroll along the shop-lined street, you peer into the windows, watching the shopkeepers and workers get ready for the day. But before you can walk more than half a block, an alert appears on your phone. Your smart home system has completed its scan and found that a small section of your house's roof has been damaged recently—with the storm coming, this could lead to a significant leak. The 3D image on your phone shows exactly what this would look like and estimates how severe the damage would be. With a few taps on your phone, the system automatically finds and pairs you with a remote technician, who inspects the virtual model of your house, finds the exact location of the leak, and schedules a drone-deployed repair robot to cover the damaged section within the hour—effectively preventing your roof from leaking during the storm.

As you pass a flower shop, your phone chimes with another alert that once again stops you in your tracks. It's your sister's birthday. You've seen it approaching on your calendar for weeks, and managed to put off finding a gift until now, at the last minute. But, in fact, you're in luck because the alert that reminded you about her birthday was generated by a sophisticated marketing platform used by the flower shop in front of you. Your sister shops at other stores that use the same platform and has opted in to share her preferences. Because the marketing platform is used by millions and millions of customers and businesses alike, it has access to vast amounts of data, all of which are shared. So it knows quite a bit—it knows, for instance, that you and your sister are related, that today is her birthday, that you usually buy her a gift on her birthday, that she likes flowers, and that you happen to be walking past a flower shop at this very moment. The flower shop, it turns out, has a surplus of orchids, and has enlisted the marketing platform to promote them. Based on your location data, the platform then served up a personalized discount voucher, suggesting the orchid as a birthday gift, and giving you 50 percent off. You run inside to make the purchase before continuing on to work.

Before long, you arrive at the small business you've run for the last ten years. You sit down at your desk and begin your day by logging on to the small business services platform you've used from the very beginning, an all-in-one portal that combines administrative services, accounting, IT, and more. The portal does just about everything you need as a small business, forecasting your cashflow, finding you the best banking providers, and connecting you directly to a consumer marketing platform—the same platform, as it happens, that just saved you the embarrassment of forgetting your sister's birthday. For the past few weeks, you've been accumulating some excess inventory for one of your products so you decide launch a marketing campaign. Now you're on the other side of the equation. Drawing on your past sales history and other data shared with your small business services platform, its advanced AI determines a pool of high-likelihood buyers. Based on their location data, shopping patterns, and any number of other variables it tracks, the platform will target this group with a personalized offer at the right time, in the right place, with the right personal message, delivered through the right channel—just like the one you received earlier in the morning. So for the next few days, just as the flower shop was able to target you in such a narrow, personalized way, you will be able to target customers who are perfectly suited to your products.

With just a few keystrokes, the campaign begins. The whole process is done in minutes.

ECOSYSTEM GROWTH WILL CONTINUE

All of this may sound a bit fantastical, but a day like this really will be possible in the not-too-distant future. As we have discussed already, the speed at which ecosystems are reshaping the world around us will only continue to increase. The massive changes that have taken place in recent years are just the beginning. Before long, ecosystems will give us more power and convenience than we ever thought possible. They will also upend the global economy, bringing huge opportunities— and a great deal of risk.

Standing on the cusp of such a major wave of changes, it behooves us to think seriously about how the future of ecosystems will unfold— and what we can do to get ready. We should start, however, by stipulating that we do not have a crystal ball to tell us exactly what will happen. We tend to agree with the famous quotation, often attributed to Mark Twain or Yogi Berra, but actually of unknown origin: "It is dangerous to make predictions—especially about the future."[1] Because predicting the future is such fraught business, we want to be careful in doing so. This means being very clear about what we can and can't predict. Trying to pinpoint with certainty specific events or developments in the future is a fool's errand. Still, having even just an approximate sense of what may happen can be incredibly useful, and it is worth our time to think about how we can productively make educated guesses.

Let's begin by making some educated guesses about the two trends that we explored in the previous chapter: the acceleration of technological innovation and the rapidly shifting behavior of consumers. It's true that there has been some variability to the forward progress of technology—and, of course, this will continue in the future. There have been slowdowns and rapid breakthroughs—and both are difficult to predict. Going forward, we expect the acceleration of progress to continue, but it's exceedingly difficult to predict exactly how that will unfold. There are, for example, developments on the horizon that promise to speed the pace of technological improvement even more—or even to redefine how computers work and what they're capable of. For example, researchers have been making astounding breakthroughs in the field of quantum computing, and in the coming years, it's likely we will see quantum computers boost the capabilities of artificial intelligence and machine learning to unprecedented levels.[2] At the same time, entrepreneurs and technologists are working hard to create a new, decentralized internet—often called Web 3.0—which could drive down costs even more while simultaneously improving security and privacy.[3]

Regardless of the potential variability of progress, what is clear is that the technological trends we have been seeing for decades now are likely to continue, especially insofar as they contribute to the development and proliferation of ecosystems. The upshot is that the borders between different sectors of the economy will continue to blur or break down, granting more and more people access to the convenience and power of ecosystems. It will be even cheaper for companies to collect and manipulate data, and even cheaper for them to create new, holistic end-to-end journeys for their customers.

But technological progress is just one of the two forces driving the emergence of ecosystems. We must also consider how consumer behavior will continue to change in the future. Here, too, the answer is fairly clear: the basic human needs that shape our participation in economic activity are unlikely to change dramatically. Every incentive will continue to push us toward ecosystem offerings. And to the extent that our behavior will evolve, it is likely to continue evolving in the same direction it has thus far—in other words, in ways that will make people more and more amenable to ecosystem offerings, and more expectant of the convenience they bring. As we considered in the previous chapter, when consumers experience a new level of convenience in one area, they will quickly come to expect it in other areas as well.

So when consumers become accustomed to ordering products online by voice through a smart speaker, they will soon come to expect that same level of convenience from, say, a bank or an insurance provider. Humans will continue to value having their needs met quickly, easily, and all together as part of a single, seamless experience. Consequently, they will continue to reward businesses and platforms that are able to cross the boundaries between different sectors of the economy—and leverage technology to provide a fully integrated experience.

Looking at the big picture, we can say with confidence that ecosystems will become a more and more dominant force in society. The question is not *if* ecosystems will grow—but rather, what will they look like? What will they grow *into*? Beyond technology and consumer trends, there are many other variables that we can examine to help us answer these questions—variables like sustainability efforts, the direction of global geopolitics, and debates over the regulation of data. We will come back to these questions and their effects on the growth of ecosystems later in the chapter. But let us first begin by considering what the coming future of ecosystems will look like on a most basic level. If the borders between sectors are fading away, what structure will take their place? How will the emerging world of ecosystems be organized?

EMERGING ECOSYSTEMS

Based on the insights we've gleaned thus far from studying the trajectory of technological progress and other trends, we can make some educated guesses about what ecosystems will look like as they continue to emerge. But these insights by themselves are not enough. To truly get a sense of how ecosystems will evolve, and what the economy will look like as the borders between sectors continue to disappear, we need something more. The driving principle of ecosystems is that they are built around customers—they fulfill customers' needs and desires on a deep level. This stands in sharp contrast to the old, sector-based economy, in which needs were understood according to the historical divisions between industries. Therefore, if we are to gain a full sense of what ecosystems will look like in the future, we must first consider what psychology can tell us about human needs.

As anyone who has taken an introductory psychology course knows, human needs are one of the field's central areas of study—and as such, enormous amounts of time and attention have been devoted to understanding them. Out of this wealth of research has emerged a number of different systems for classifying and organizing human needs, some more astute than others. Perhaps the most familiar is the American psychologist Abraham Maslow's hierarchy of needs, a framework that he described in a 1943 academic paper, "A Theory of Human Motivation."[4] His classification of needs is usually depicted in the form of pyramid, and presumes that the fulfillment of more basic needs like sustenance and safety are a prerequisite for the fulfillment of higher-order needs like self-esteem and intellectual curiosity.

But while Maslow's hierarchy is popular and widely studied for good reason, it's not the right tool for analyzing the intersection of businesses and human needs. For this purpose, we prefer a framework proposed by the Chilean economist Manfred Max-Neef. While work-ing as an economics professor at several different universities, includ-ing at the University of California, Berkeley, Max-Neef traveled extensively throughout Latin America, studying and spending time among impoverished communities. A few years later, in 1986, he wrote an article in which he sketched out a new way of organizing what he called fundamental needs—which include subsistence, protection, affection, understanding, participation, idleness, creation, identity, and freedom.[5]

At their core, ecosystems form around human needs and desires. The boundaries between different sectors of the economy arose from logistical concerns not related to human needs and desires. The rise of ecosystems, therefore, is the expression of what humans really want—made possible through advances in technology and organization. So in the future, as technology continues to improve, we will see human needs and desires expressed more and more clearly in the organization of ecosystems.

Although it's very difficult to predict exactly what this will look like, we believe it is worth taking the time to consider one possibility of how these ecosystems might develop as industries continue to con-solidate into new formations. Rather than a prediction, we might think of this as an imaginative exercise to help us better understand the momentous changes that this reorganization will bring.

From the Max-Neef framework, we can extrapolate some spe-cific and concrete ways that human needs translate to consumer behaviors, and from these we can glimpse some ecosystems that may be forming—or may form in the future (see Figure 3.1). To do this, we begin with a handful of the most pertinent fundamental

FIGURE 3.1 **How fundamental needs connect with derived needs that inform potential ecosystem evolution**

FUNDAMENTAL NEED	DERIVED NEED	ECOSYSTEM

INDIVIDUAL

- Subsistence → Essentials, products
- Idleness → Recreation / Experiences
- Survival → Adaptability, moving
- Subsistence → Physical and mental well-being
- Protection → Peace of mind, long-term stability
- Creation/understanding → Meaning, role in community/gov't
- Affection/protection → Shelter

INSTITUTIONAL

- Reaching customers → Selling and marketing
- Acquiring and retaining talent → Human resources management
- Obtaining supply/inputs → Procurement
- Optimizing operations → Operational expertise
- Making long-term decisions → Strategic thinking
- Attaining physical assets → Asset management
- Accessing capital and liquidity → Financial services
- Being accountable to stakeholders → Regulatory and legal

Ecosystems: Commerce, Travel, Digital Experience, Mobility, Health, Wealth & Stability, Talent, Home, SME Services, Input Marketplace, Enterprise Services, Community & Government needs from Max-Neef's framework: subsistence, survival, protection, affection, idleness, creation, and understanding. From these we can derive a set of more practical needs, directly related to our consumer behaviors as individuals—and these, in turn, can show us what ecosystems we might expect to see in the future. So, for example, from the fundamental need for subsistence would follow derived needs like the need for essentials for survival, or the need for physical and mental well-being. From the need for essentials for survival, we can theorize a commerce ecosystem. From the need for physical and mental well-being, we can project a health ecosystem. Similarly, from a fundamental need like the need for protection, we can derive the practical need for shelter—encompassing decisions like where to live or which house to buy—and from this we can theorize the emergence of an ecosystem centered on finding a home. Similarly, from the fundamental need for idleness would follow derived needs like the need for recreation or the need for experience—and from these we can theorize ecosystems centered on travel and digital experience.

Of course, the needs of businesses and other organizations will also play a role in shaping the ecosystems of the future, so these must be considered, as well. Manfred Max-Neef did not extend his analysis into the needs of organizations, but they are not difficult to determine—businesses, after all, are made up of humans working together toward a common goal. So what are the fundamental needs that, if satisfied, allow businesses and organizations to get things done and find success? So far as we can tell, these include needs for customers, human capital, access to inputs and conversion, optimizing operations, short-term and long-term planning, physical assets, governance, and accountability. Again, as with individual needs, we can derive from these a set of more practical needs, which in turn can be used to identify a handful of emerging ecosystems. So from the fundamental organizational need for customers, say, we can derive more practical needs like the need for human resources, legal, sales, and marketing functions, and from these we can extrapolate the emergence of an ecosystem centered on services for small and medium enterprises (SMEs)—which we call the SME Services ecosystem. From the fundamental need for human capital, we can derive more practical needs like the need for talent acquisition and management functions—and from these we can project the formation of an education and talent ecosystem.

Based on all of these fundamental needs and derived needs, it seems plausible to us that, in the future, ecosystems will coalesce around a number of different categories, spanning both business-to-business (B2B) and business-to-consumer (B2C) offerings. We can begin to map out what some of these might be: wealth and protection, public services, health, education, entertainment, housing, mobility, travel and hospitality, the B2C marketplace, the B2B marketplace, B2B services, and global corporate services. As you'll see in Figure 3.2 that follows, certain ecosystems involve multiple different fundamental and derived needs. In any case, each of these ecosystems, if it comes to pass, will follow its own course of development and find expression in its own way. We have chosen these twelve ecosystems in particular because they follow logically from the Max-Neef framework, but it is important to remember that this is not by any means a comprehensive accounting. Many other ecosystems may emerge—this is just a sampling.

In fact, we have already seen some of these twelve ecosystems forming in recent years as industries, responding to technological and consumer changes, have begun converging under newer, broader, and more dynamic alignments. In the future, these groupings could continue to consolidate even faster and more decisively. It is important to note that this is just one way that ecosystems may develop—many others are possible. There are also many subtleties and nuances that are not fully expressed in these groupings—for example, as we will explore later, these ecosystems, which we also call macro-ecosystems, frequently contain smaller and more localized ecosystems, called micro-ecosystems, which in turn contain their own smaller and more localized ecosystems, called sub-ecosystems. In any case, the twelve macro-ecosystems do not constitute a durable formation—they will surely continue to evolve as the economy changes over time, and as human needs change over time, responding to future events that are far beyond our power to predict.

Each of these emerging ecosystems will offer a substantial prize to the winners, with expected multi-trillion-dollar revenue pools being orchestrated by the top platforms by 2030. The profitability of these new battlefields will vary substantially, of course, somewhat offsetting the revenue differences—we expect that each of the new ecosystems will have profit pools between $0.5 trillion and $1.5 trillion by the end of the decade, a tremendous upside to be captured by a selected group of winners (see Figure 3.2).

FIGURE 3.2   **A potential evolution of ecosystem economy**

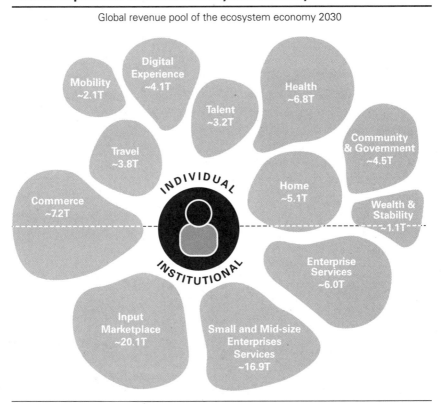

Global revenue pool of the ecosystem economy 2030

In Figure 3.3, you can begin to see how some of these ecosystems that are forming might fit together. But what will they look like? Figure 3.4 describes how we imagine them taking shape. It is unavoidable that some of these descriptions may sound very similar to traditional sectors that have focused on the same needs—for example, the real estate sector has a great deal of overlap with the home/shelter ecosystem. But ecosystems are, of course, more dynamic formations that work best when they are crossing the boundaries between traditional sectors of the economy, and we have tried to emphasize throughout how they differ from the compartmentalized sectors that preceded them.

To demonstrate the power that these new ecosystems will hold, let's examine just one of them in a bit more detail. Take the education and talent ecosystem, for example. In the future, as the borders between

FIGURE 3.3 **Each ecosystem is connected to several others**

Ecosystems group distinct holistic needs, and several relevant sub-ecosystems can be found within their domain, connecting them with other adjacent ecosystems.

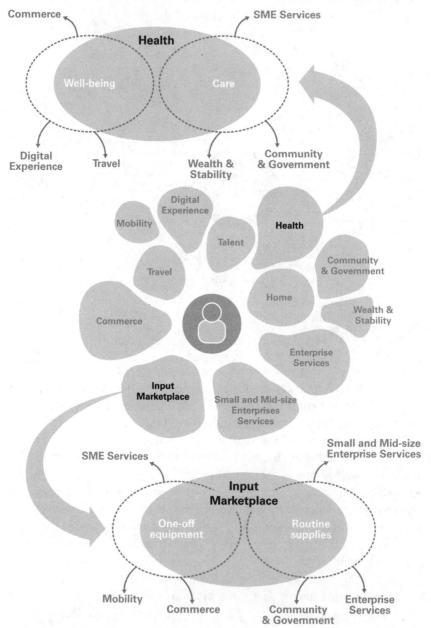

FIGURE 3.4 **The twelve emerging ecosystems**

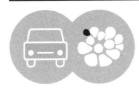

Mobility

Frequently used personal mobility-related solutions and services, including: vehicle purchase and maintenance management, ridesharing, carpooling, public transport, traffic management, vehicle connectivity.

Home

Covering the complete journeys of property purchase, rental, and investments, including: property search, financing, legal and admin services, refurbishment, design, moving to maintenance.

Digital Experience

Complete range of direct or user-generated digital content, including: audio, video, images, news, advertisements and interactive digital entertainment services like social media, gaming, gambling.

Talent

Educational solutions for compulsory, voluntary, and life-long learning, including: interactive, personalized learning aids, digital educational content.

Health

Integrated personal health, medicine, and wellness services offering personalized treatment, remote support, personalized medications, insurance, fitness solutions.

Travel

Digitized, platform-based (digital and non-digital) hospitality, accommodation and travel services, including: online hotel booking, peer-to-peer (P2P) accommodations, long-haul land based, water and air travel, entertainment, restaurants.

(Continued)

FIGURE 3.4 **The twelve emerging ecosystems (*Continued*)**

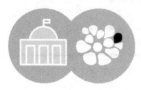

Community & Government

Government services (digital and non-digital), including: social security and other centralized administrative services.

Wealth & Stability

Long-term saving and financial protection needs, aggregation into a single digital offering; includes existing personal financial services, such as asset management, life insurance, private banking.

Enterprise Services

Large corporate business operations-related service needs. Targets truly global business needs, and thus, includes M&A, treasury, large-scale IT services, strategy consulting.

Small and Mid-size Enterprise Services

SME business operations-related service needs, including: bookkeeping, invoicing, business administration, payroll, legal, tax, business travel, and business intelligence services.

Input Marketplace

Fulfillment of B2B needs for purchasing goods throughout the supply chain, ranging from supply management, financing, transactions, warehousing, transportation to demand planning, production management, and predictive maintenance.

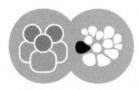

Commerce

Addressing (retail) purchasing needs through digital and physical marketplaces with goods and services; offered in a seamless package of: payments solutions, consumer loans, loyalty programs, logistics, CRM/sales management for businesses.

sectors continue to disappear, we will see parts of the education, job market, and digital content areas converge into a new ecosystem, in which digital platforms connect all of these functions into integrated, seamless customer propositions. These propositions will create an explosion of new and more varied options for learning, personal growth, entertainment, and finding a job. In all likelihood, education and talent ecosystem players will partner with traditional educational institutions, like schools—and will end up completely changing the way they operate. The school system as we know it, from grade school through university and beyond, will be transformed—with a much broader range of degrees offered, and a much more extensive set of remote learning possibilities. With the power to offer more immersive and personalized online, remote learning options (as is already happening with companies like Coursera), the largest and most prestigious colleges and universities will be able to reach a much larger audience of students. Those without the fame or recognition to pull off such an arrangement will likely struggle.

But the platforms operated by education and talent ecosystem players will run far beyond the traditional education system as well. Alongside university courses, users of all ages will have the opportunity to gain practical skills and obtain licenses or certifications. Imagine getting your driver's license or a CPR certification from the same app through which you take a university-level history course. These platforms will also increasingly blur the lines between education and entertainment, offering a marketplace of educational content from highly engaging creators who will compete with one another for students. Sophisticated algorithms will optimize the experience for everyone involved, continually monitoring students' interests and skills, pairing them with other students at a similar level, and providing a highly personalized, individually tailored learning experience. Critically, ecosystems will also connect to the job market, using their deep, individual knowledge of students' skills, strengths, weaknesses, and achievements to pair them with jobs to which they are perfectly suited. And this will not stop after a person finds their first job—rather, the ecosystem will offer a wide range of long-term, life-long learning options, helping workers to advance through their careers and even providing enrichment activities for retirees.

This is just one example of how, in the future, different sectors will converge into ecosystems that meet customer needs holistically. Going forward, companies will have to think carefully about where they fit into this landscape, and how they can adjust their operations to play more competitively in whatever ecosystem they decide to pursue. Some companies, however, may find that they are best at serving consumer needs that don't fit neatly within a single ecosystem—needs that are more specialized or particular. These companies will find that they are playing in what we call micro-ecosystems. Whereas the macro-ecosystems that we have been exploring encompass broad constellations of different-but-related customer needs, micro-ecosystems are more narrowly focused, and frequently cut across the boundaries of macro-ecosystems.

We expect that these micro-ecosystems, however, will exist in a state of flux, and will be organized not around our basic human needs but around needs that may prove more transient. We can identify some of them, but they will shift—more rapidly than macro-ecosystems—as circumstances change over the years, causing some to fade away and others to take their place.

Now that we have explored some of the ecosystems that may develop in the future, their enormous potential is hopefully becoming clear. So far, humanity has only scratched the surface of what they can deliver. As we continue trying to understand where ecosystems may go in the future, we will need to think carefully about the various drivers shaping ecosystem evolution—that is to say, about the factors that could potentially affect their trajectory, shape, and size. Although there are many such factors, we will focus our thinking here by narrowing in on a handful of the most important ones—including the shifting geopolitical landscape; regulation (including especially the regulation of data); the need to address climate change; and possible accelerations in AI, cybersecurity, space propulsion technology, biotechnology, and nanotechnology.

GEOPOLITICS

Let us begin with geopolitics. Although there are a vast number of different directions that geopolitics could take us, and many layers of nuance, at the heart of the matter is a binary question: Will the world become more globalized or more regionalized?

Over the course of the twentieth century, the world became more and more interconnected as new technological advancements made international trade more efficient. In the aftermath of World War II, a series of international agreements championed by the US and other countries helped to spur transnational trade to new levels. Then, in the late twentieth century, with the fall of the Soviet Union, the creation of the World Trade Organization, and the rise of the internet, the process of globalization continued with even greater energy. According to a report from the World Economic Forum, the result was "globalization on steroids. In the 2000s, global exports reached a milestone, as they rose to about a quarter of global GDP. Trade, the sum of imports and exports, consequentially grew to about half of world GDP. . . . A majority of the global population has benefited from this: more people than ever before belong to the global middle class, and hundreds of millions achieved that status by participating in the global economy."[6]

But as the twentieth century gave way to the twenty-first, many politicians and ordinary people across the world began to grow skeptical of the benefits of globalization. As the World Economic Forum report continues: "In the West particularly, many middle-class workers are fed up with a political and economic system that resulted in economic inequality, social instability, and—in some countries—mass immigration, even if it also led to economic growth and cheaper products. Protectionism, trade wars and immigration stops are once again the order of the day in many countries." This increasing malaise has even occasionally spilled over into warlike posturing between old rivals and ideological adversaries.[7]

Looking to the future, it is difficult to say what the fate of globalization will be. Will we see a resurgence of internationalism and cooperation among the different nations of the world? Will we perhaps even see a strengthening of international organizations like the European Union and the United Nations, and of free trade agreements? Or will we see countries continuing to turn inward, building nationalist political coalitions, and raising the temperature on long-simmering ideological conflicts, perhaps even leading to war?

Much will depend on the answers to these questions. In the case of a more peaceful, internationalist world, we are likely to see much more cooperation and trade between countries, and it will thus be easier for companies to operate in many different markets, leveraging even larger pools of data to serve customer needs. In the case of a more inward-looking, nationalist world, we will see more companies and ecosystems operating exclusively within certain regions or countries, and developing specifically to fit the needs of that region. This would in many ways mirror the situation today in a country like China, where the government's Great Firewall has kept out many Western ecosystem players, and where a handful of powerful but regionally specific players compete for customer ownership in the domestic market.

To more closely examine the consequences for ecosystems, we will imagine just one possible outcome. Let us suppose that the world becomes more fragmented and regionalized, with each country or geographical area taking its own path. In such a world, international trade would suffer as national boundaries become increasingly hardened and contentious, rather than open and free. This is a scenario that might come to pass if, for example, there is a flare-up in relations between the US and China, precipitating a new Cold War. We could imagine in such a war that global trade would be severely disrupted and that cyber-attacks between the different warring parties would constantly bleed into civilian life and disrupt economic activity.

But there are many different forms that such a fracturing could take—it would not necessarily mean a simple West-versus-East split. It may be that as China continues its ascent, the rest of the world will come together to some degree in an effort to curb its power. There may a complicated rebalancing in which a handful of Asian countries like India and Japan come together to challenge China's power in the East Asian world, while North America and the European Union take separate paths. It's also possible that, instead of a clear-cut answer on the binary question of globalization versus regionalization, we will see a world where somewhat different models coexist—in which certain regions and countries are culturally open and economically integrated with the global community while others are more isolated.

Whatever form it takes, though, such a scenario of a fractured geopolitical environment would have a drastic effect on the size, shape, and scope of potential ecosystems. Even as they gain incredible powers by climbing to the top of the hill in their own country or region, companies would face steep—and likely prohibitive—challenges in any attempt to expand elsewhere. Beyond just a high base-level cost of doing business internationally, companies would have to contend with a tangle of regulatory and governmental barriers. Many countries would likely impose bans on doing business in specific countries due to ideological tensions—or even open conflicts.

With such imposing barriers to operating in many different countries, it's likely that few ecosystem players would be able to extend their reach into nearly every corner of the world. As such, each country would grow its own technology platform titans. Ecosystem-based competition within countries or regions would be intense, but almost nonexistent internationally.

MAJOR REGULATORY CHANGES

The direction of geopolitics is one of the most important drivers of ecosystem evolution, but another will be the direction of regulatory practices—particularly regulation of data. Here's why: as the borders between traditional sectors continue to fade in the coming years, companies will find themselves locked in intense competition, not just with their traditional rivals, but also with players they never expected to face. Their success or failure will be measured not by market share but by customer ownership. And to win on that front, data will be of utmost importance. We therefore expect that the current rush to acquire more and more data will only intensify as time wears on. What's far less certain is what the rules governing the use of that data will be. Will we live in a world of shared data, where companies are obliged by governments to share their data with others—or a world where data is owned by a concentrated set of players?

To answer that question, let's begin with another: Who owns the data? The answer is obvious: we do. The people do. The data we are talking about are data *about us*, generated by us—whether they are data about your genetics (which might be useful to health ecosystem players) or data about your shopping habits (which may be useful to commerce players). The question before us is a question of how that ownership will be regulated and what policies will be built around it. There are all sorts of wildly different views on this. Some observers point out that consumers are willingly signing away the rights to their data when they sign up for services, like social media platforms, which collect and monetize it. These platforms, of course, are free—people are getting something in return for their data. So, the argument goes, while the data may have been theirs to begin with, they've bartered it away. Others say that big companies are tricking consumers into giving up too much for too little in return, and these critics advocate forcing companies to pay consumers a monetary sum in exchange for their data.

However, the larger—though related—question that this gets at is whether data should be shared or owned by a concentrated set of players. If customers are the true and rightful owners of their data, why should any one company have more of a claim to those data than the others? Some analysts and policymakers believe that governments should require companies to share their data with others through open Application Programming Interfaces (or open APIs), making data more of an open resource, or a utility, than a privileged commodity that companies keep to themselves. Doing so, they say, would boost innovation by allowing any startup or competitor the chance to build a more effective value proposition using the same data that incumbents enjoy. One example of this philosophy in action is the regulation of European banks. In 2015, the EU adopted the Revised Payment Services Directive (known as PSD2), which among other things required banks to share customer data securely with third parties, where it could be accessed by other financial institutions.[8] The goal was to give customers more autonomy over their data and to encourage more innovation and competition between banks by levelling the playing field. In the years since then, the regulatory shift has had less of an impact than many analysts predicted, but it still forced banks to improve their propositions by accelerating competition—they could no longer sit comfortably on their stockpiles of data. It also offers insight into, and a possible model for, how a larger-scale open data framework might function in the future.[9]

The outcome of this shared-or-concentrated debate will have enormous consequences for how the economy will be organized in the future—and for the future of ecosystems. If future data regulators tend toward a more concentrated model, and companies are left to hoard their data, the advantages of incumbency would be greatly amplified, which in turn would set off a sort of arms race for data: whichever company is able to accumulate the most data the fastest would win the coveted spot as the most powerful ecosystem player, and it would be extremely difficult for any competitor to oust them. Consequently, we would likely see a small handful of companies growing more and more powerful—to the point that it may become quite difficult for smaller players to compete. On the other hand, if the data regulators in the future tend toward a shared model, we would be likely to see a constant churn of new companies starting, taking off, and failing in rapid succession. Small and large players would compete side by side on a more-or-less level playing field, and everyone would be required to share their data, which would function more like a utility than a proprietary resource.

As a thought experiment, let us consider the implications of this latter scenario. It seems highly likely that, in the future, customers will enjoy a healthy degree of privacy and will be given license to control how their data are used. The question is how those data will be regulated once they are in the hands of companies. Let us suppose, then, a scenario in which a shared-data policy like the EU's PSD2 spreads across the world—a scenario in which many different governments, in relatively short order, come around to the idea that forcing companies to share their data through open APIs would facilitate competition and innovation. In such a scenario, companies would find themselves engaged in fierce battles against one another— centered not on which of them can accumulate data the fastest, but rather on which can devise the best value propositions, and design the best customer experiences. These companies would face stiff competition not only from their traditional rivals but from startups as well. Even though incumbents would enjoy considerable advantages stemming from their global reach and their sheer size, the government-imposed regime of open APIs would give newcomers a powerful weapon with which to fight back. Building on some of the existing capabilities of their incumbent rivals, startups would be free to pursue creative and unorthodox new strategies with a much lower barrier to entry than new companies face today. We could see powerful new players pop up seemingly overnight.

But even in such a case, if a broader and more universally applicable version of PSD2 were to catch on globally, it still seems likely that different regions would have different outcomes. This is because many countries and governments have drastically different fundamental philosophies about the relationship between individuals and society. We can imagine that regions, like the European Union, that have traditionally favored a social-democratic form of governance, and a stronger role for the state, would be more inclined to support such a policy of enforced data-sharing. More individualist societies like the US are also likely to promote individuals' ownership of their data and strong privacy protections, but they may be more inclined to pursue that goal through traditional forms of regulation. Countries like China, in which government surveillance and censorship are widespread and expected, may take an entirely different path—customers may not have autonomy over their data, but those data would sooner be controlled by the government than private interests.

All of these different outcomes will have an important effect on how ecosystems evolve in different parts of the world and will play a vital role in determining which players will be successful in developing ecosystems. In regions that adopt a system of forced data sharing, we may in a few decades see a new generation of ecosystem-driven tech platforms rising up and, in some cases, displacing incumbents—so long as they can overcome the advantages that incumbents hold by virtue of being the first movers. In regions that favor a more traditional, less interventionist, approach to data regulation, there is a higher chance that we will see many of the same players that are dominating the field today. Incumbent players that have a first-mover advantage will be well positioned to concentrate their advantage and achieve a network effect, making it ever more difficult for new players.

ENVIRONMENT, SOCIAL, AND GOVERNANCE (ESG)

Another factor that will have a significant influence on the development of ecosystems is climate change. Much as we might wish the situation were different, the reality is that climate change is already happening—we are already seeing daily life disrupted by extreme weather events. Experts predict that, despite our best efforts, temperatures will continue to climb and weather events like hurricanes, droughts, wildfires, and floods will become more extreme, more frequent, and more unpredictable. There is much uncertainty about how fast this will happen, how severe the effects will be, and how quickly and decisively humanity will respond. According to a recent analysis by scientists at the research group Climate Action Tracker, the 2020s are "a make-or-break opportunity to avoid the most devastating impacts of climate change and steer the world towards a net-zero future." Following the 2014 Paris Climate Accords, humanity has made notable progress in the effort to limit carbon and other emissions and to mitigate the most harmful environmental consequences. But, as the Climate Action Tracker report makes clear, we are still not doing enough: "It is still possible to limit global warming to 1.5 degrees C (2.7 degrees F)"—the level widely understood as necessary to stave off the most catastrophic effects of climate change—but doing so "will require rapid, far-reaching transformations across every sector—from power, buildings, industry and transport to land-use, coastal zone management and agriculture—as well as the immediate scale-up of carbon removal and climate finance."[10]

Regardless of how exactly humanity responds to this crisis, it will play an important role in shaping ecosystems. But in order to further our thinking, let us suppose for a moment that we are able to do what's necessary—that all across the world, from China to India, to the US, to Russia, there is a groundswell of support for immediate and meaningful action on climate change and sustainability. Let us suppose that there is more progress in the next several years than there has been in the last fifteen years—that humanity collectively recognizes the severity of the dilemma we're facing and overcomes old ideological divides to collaborate on solutions that truly meet the moment.

The effort needed to accomplish this goal would be enormous, and would have a profound influence both on how society is organized—and on the development of ecosystems. As the borders between traditional sectors of the economy continue to dissolve, sustainability efforts are likely both to shape existing ecosystems and to become a dynamic proving ground for new ones. In fact, chances are that we will see a whole micro-ecosystem form dedicated to mitigating the effects of climate change and helping consumers to do their part by making more conscientious decisions. Micro-ecosystems, we will recall, frequently cut across several or more of the broader, macro-ecosystems—and that would certainly be the case with this climate-focused micro-ecosystem. In fact, the sustainability efforts necessary to get to 1.5°C will be so broad and multi-faceted that even this micro-ecosystem would be likely to contain a number of different sub-ecosystems. (By a sub-ecosystem, we mean an even smaller and more localized ecosystem within a micro-ecosystem.) Some efforts may center on planting trees and enabling people to track the potential environmental impact of products they are buying or investments they are making—while others may focus on technologies like carbon capture, a process by which carbon dioxide is removed from emissions or from the atmosphere and either recycled or stored.

Another potential sub-ecosystem may form around lab-grown meat. Today, methane emissions from cattle are among the most significant contributors to climate change—and in response, many environmentalists have reasonably called for reducing our meat consumption.[11] However, another solution that has received considerable attention as of late is the prospect of using recent advances in biotechnology to grow artificial meat in a lab—meat which would be essentially indistinguishable from the meat we eat today, but would not require the slaughter of animals. Public opinion surveys have thus far shown limited interest in such an alternative, but many are betting that the prospect of drastically cutting down on both animal cruelty and greenhouse gas emissions will be enough to persuade skeptical consumers to look past what may initially seem to be an unpalatable option. Scientists and entrepreneurs alike have begun placing considerable energy and resources into making it a reality—but almost everyone agrees that more research is needed.[12] Once these issues are settled, the formation of a sub-ecosystem may be the final push needed to make lab-grown meat a reality. For lab-grown meat to be produced at scale and truly make a difference would also require close collaboration between the biotechnology and agriculture industries—an ideal opening for an ecosystem play.

ARTIFICIAL INTELLIGENCE BREAKTHROUGH

In this chapter, we began by examining the variables we can predict with some degree of certainty: technology and consumer trends, both of which point overwhelmingly to the continued expansion of ecosystems and the continued blurring of borders between traditional sectors of the economy. We then moved on to less certain variables, like geopolitics and data regulation, which may have a profound effect on how those ecosystems develop, but are more challenging to predict. There are, however, a number of other more extreme drivers that have the potential to bring about even more exaggerated outcomes. Perhaps one of the most important lessons that history teaches us is that unlikely and seemingly farfetched possibilities often turn out to be the most consequential. We ignore them at our own peril.

One such driver could be a breakthrough in artificial intelligence technology that leads us to achieve what's called true AI, or AI with human-like capabilities. Although AI researchers and developers have accomplished extraordinary things in recent years, the objective of true AI remains further out. According to the technology reporter James Vincent, "to date, we've built countless systems that are superhuman at specific tasks, but none that can match a rat when it comes to general brain power." Vincent goes on to cite a recent survey of leading technology researchers, in which they predict it's unlikely we will achieve true AI until around the year 2100.[13]

It is, however, conceivable that AI researchers may make some discovery that drastically accelerates their work and that, as a consequence,

we may achieve true AI much sooner, perhaps in the next several decades. If this were to happen, the implications for ecosystem evolution
would be enormous. Some ecosystems where the advances in AI could
be quickly and efficiently applied would see a massive acceleration.
The mobility ecosystem, for example, would likely see rapid progress
since true AI would probably spur a revolution in autonomous driving
technology. In the social networking space, too, we would see a rapid
expansion of possibilities as AI takes platforms like the metaverse to
unprecedented and unimaginable levels. It's also likely that many ecosystems would increase in size as AI power helps to free up their
capacity. Others would use the new power to pursue brand-new ecosystem plays, either creating their own micro-ecosystems from new
applications of AI, or finding new positions within existing ecosystems. It's possible, for example, that AI-powered ecosystems would
lead to a scenario in which every human would have their own, personalized AI program attending to their needs, helping them navigate
areas ranging from health care, to food shopping, to small business
administration. All together, such an AI breakthrough would elicit a
whirlwind of economic activity that would open important new ave-
nues for ecosystem growth.

THE METAVERSE

Another important driver that will shape the future of ecosystems is
the growth and evolution of the metaverse. The metaverse, which
we've already referred to, is an immersive digital environment that
leverages augmented reality (AR), virtual reality (VR), and extended
reality (XR) technologies to connect people, businesses, and other
institutions. A number of companies are working in the metaverse,
building capabilities that range from gaming to remote conferencing
to social networking. One difficulty it presents is its definition—the
metaverse means different things to different people. However, one
explanation offered by the venture capitalist Matthew Ball has proven
influential. As Ball writes, the metaverse is "an expansive network of
persistent, real-time rendered 3D worlds and simulations that support continuity of identity, objects, history, payments, and entitle-
ments, and can be experienced synchronously by an effectively
unlimited number of users, each with an individual sense of
presence."[14]

Much of the promise of the metaverse has yet to be fulfilled, but the energy behind it is mounting, and flocks of businesses and would-be entrepreneurs are already exploring ways to leverage its capabilities. When that happens, there will be significant consequences for the evolution of ecosystems. Perhaps even more so than current internet and mobile-app-based ecosystem platforms, the metaverse stands to serve as a powerful means of integrating different businesses and services into a streamlined value proposition that serves customer needs holistically. Rather than navigating between different applications on a mobile interface, users will be able to move seamlessly with their avatars through a digital environment, interacting with different business offerings, choosing and comparing services, and making purchases.

In this sense, the metaverse could become an ecosystem in and of itself, spawning a multitude of micro- and sub-ecosystems. It could also become a backbone or an enabler for some of the biggest and most established ecosystems currently in existence—imagine, for example, today's largest online commerce ecosystems integrating all of their services and offerings, and all of their third-party providers, within an immersive, interactive experience. Shoppers could examine AR/VR digital twins of products before buying them or could use a virtual fitting room to try on clothes. Or consider the consequences for the mobility ecosystem—to take just one, vehicle maintenance and repair could be completely transformed if every car company made AR/VR digital twins available to technicians through the metaverse. On the whole, if the metaverse continues to expand and flourish as it seems likely to, it will become both an important catalyst for ecosystem growth and an integral part of how so many of today's ecosystems operate.

WEB 3.0

The metaverse, however, isn't the only transformative new vision of digital connectivity. Many technologists and businesspeople are talking about what is called Web 3.0, or Web3. Though it is often loosely defined, Web 3.0 is a decentralized version of the internet, where systems from social networks to marketplaces are not governed by top-down hierarchies in the way that much of the internet's current infrastructure and leading companies are. In place of these hierarchies or other top-down infrastructure, Web 3.0 and its constituent parts are organized and powered by what is called the blockchain, a decentralized system that uses computers in different locations to keep a collective and publicly available record of certain data, like transaction records.[15] Blockchain also underpins cryptocurrencies like Bitcoin. As you might intuit, Web 3.0 follows from Web 1.0, which refers to the early days of the internet in the 1990s when email, chat, and basic browsing were some of the most advanced functions that any significant number of people could use. Web 2.0 came in the 2000s as large companies accrued more power on the internet and began to shape it more significantly, with social networks, powerful search engines, and online retail marketplaces increasing the number of users on the internet by orders of magnitude. Now Web 3.0 stands to shift some of that power to different groups and people, including especially the users themselves.

Web 3.0 presents a vast range of different opportunities to evolve current ecosystems, power them in new ways, or form new ecosystems. Today, in the realm of, say, social networking, there are a handful of dominant players, and while those players are creating an enormous amount of value, they are also capturing a substantial portion of that value. Web 3.0 opens up the possibility for that value to be distributed among a wider group and to be put to a much broader range of purposes. Its decentralized organization, moreover, raises interesting questions about how businesses will incorporate it into their ecosystems—it could even drive the creation of entirely new ecosystem structures. As it stands, we have yet to see exactly how Web 3.0 will drive ecosystem growth, but what does seem certain is that such a fundamental shift to a decentralized system will have an enormous impact on the communities of digital and physical businesses that work across sector boundaries to address customer needs holistically.

DEFI

While blockchain certainly has many wide-ranging implications for technologies like Web 3.0, it is also transforming the world of finance—and this, too, will have important consequences for the development of ecosystems. This is perhaps most apparent in the rise of what has come to be called decentralized finance, or DeFi. As an article in *Business Insider* explains, DeFi is "a global financial system that takes place on blockchains that are public." It works by essentially taking out "the middleman in financial transactions. So instead of having your bank or credit card issuer be the intermediary between you and a merchant when you make a purchase, you use the digital currency and have ownership of it to use directly."[16] As DeFi continues to grow and evolve, we will see a vastly different kind of financial system emerge. A primary purpose of financial institutions as we think of them today is to collect deposits and make loans—but what happens if those tasks can be managed through secure, low-cost, and scalable technologies like blockchain?

Even in a baseline scenario, we can expect that finance will be one of the most profoundly disrupted sectors. Not only will its distribution be disrupted, but so too will its very core value proposition and business model. And as ecosystems continue to grow and evolve alongside these developments, we are likely to see the financial sector divided and engulfed by different ecosystems. Many services that are currently folded into banking and financial services fit much more appropriately into emerging ecosystems. Mortgages, for example, have much more to do with the home/shelter ecosystem than they do with other services that a bank offers, like credit cards or savings accounts. Credit card services have much more to do with the commerce ecosystem. Car loans have much more to do with the mobility ecosystem. And so on. As DeFi weakens the financial sector's core proposition, we are likely to see many of these functions break away and become part of integrated ecosystem offerings focused on fundamental customer needs. This in itself will constitute a significant change to the structure of ecosystems. Banks that can see this coming (e.g., Sberbank and Royal Bank of Canada) are already working to become broader ecosystem orchestrators.

But in a more extreme scenario, DeFi's disruption of finance could happen so quickly and thoroughly that it would reshape ecosystems on an even broader level. First and foremost, it would radically transform the way that payments work, especially in markets where payment technology is still very traditional and outdated, like the United States. One of the most consequential outcomes of DeFi, for these markets, will be its ability to enable instantaneous, free, and secure payments from any party to any other party. At present, payment operators hold an enormous amount of power and influence, given the centrality of their offerings to so many different ecosystems—but if DeFi's disruption of the finance sector is as swift and pronounced as some are projecting, these players could be dislodged from their privileged position. Another outcome, and an even more important one, is that DeFi will change how banking balance sheets work. In place of these institutions, we would see entirely new peer-to-peer platforms and DeFi companies appear with massive customer bases, immediate broad appeal, and zero marginal costs. Because of such advantages, these players would be far more aggressive challengers to the biggest tech players than any financial institution is today. These companies would be thinner than today's banks, but they would probably also be broader, and have far fewer costs. And most importantly, they would have the foundation to become powerful ecosystem orchestrators. Ultimately, an extreme DeFi scenario could lead to the emergence of a powerful new cohort of ecosystem orchestrators, which could stand to reshape the economy as we know it.

EXTREME CYBER EVENTS

Another dimension of uncertainty that could have a huge effect on the development of ecosystems is the future of cybersecurity. Cybersecurity threats have been around just about as long as digital technology itself—and ever since then, as those threats have evolved, so too have efforts to combat them. This ever-escalating cyber arms race has continued for decades, as malicious actors and cybersecurity professionals have both developed more and more sophisticated methods of circumventing each other. What we are seeing now is that the emergence of ecosystems drastically ups the stakes of this long-simmering conflict—with end-to-end customer journeys and more and more data being shared online, the risks are getting exponentially higher. We have all seen the headlines in recent years about increasing ransomware attacks and other intrusions by malicious actors.[17] As devastating as these attacks have been for the many companies and individuals they have targeted, they are insignificant compared to the dangers on the horizon. The truth is that the scariest and most destructive possibilities have not yet come to pass.

We can imagine that in a baseline scenario, this arms race will continue on its current trajectory, without either side gaining a distinct advantage. However, more extreme scenarios are possible—perhaps even likely. In such a scenario, unfortunately, we can expect attacks to become more frequent and more extreme. According to one recent report, "computer hacks have become so frequent that they are now occurring, on average, every 39 seconds. The majority of cyberattacks are done using automated scripts that crawl through databases and digital addresses, searching for vulnerabilities to exploit."[18] And that number is only going up. We have already seen headline-grabbing attacks, but thus far, we have not seen any that have disrupted daily life for ordinary people in a major way.

As the frequency and severity of attacks increase, we could see a truly catastrophic cyber event—imagine, for example, if hackers were able to disable payment systems worldwide. Worse still, as sophisticated technologies connect more and more of the world around us to the internet, hackers and other malicious actors will find more and more ways of exploiting these connections. Think, for example, of smart home technologies, autonomous cars, or other Internet of Things (IoT) technologies. If a hacker were able to gain control of these devices, that person would have a powerful means of blackmailing users—the hacker would hold people's very lives in their hands. With just a few keystrokes, a passenger could be sent into oncoming traffic.[19] We could also see ransomware attacks on a scale many times beyond what we have seen thus far. As of yet, ransomware attacks have mostly taken place on an individual level—targeting a hospital here, or an insurance company there. In the future, however, we could see these attacks radically expanded to target millions of people and institutions simultaneously. The level of turmoil this would unleash is scarcely imaginable.[20]

If we were to experience a catastrophic global cyber event—or even just a marked acceleration of more and more sophisticated individual attacks—this could alter the development of ecosystems in a major way. For example, such an escalation may prompt governments to take an even more active role in managing cybersecurity—not just enforcing cybersecurity rules, but taking a direct and active role in carrying out the work of cybersecurity. After witnessing an extreme escalation of cyberattacks, companies, too, would have a strong incentive to make their operations as secure as possible. This will lead to new micro- and sub-ecosystems focused on security and personal encryption. Cybersecurity will become an enormous business—far beyond what we have today. Algorithms and customer data may be heavily regulated and protected. And all of this may become more centralized, as governments take a more active role and as companies and customers alike come to accept the necessity of protecting personal data behind a single, extremely secure choke point. This could lead to the emergence of extremely powerful cybersecurity companies, which would take part in every transaction and every touchpoint that a customer has online. In short, cybersecurity companies would become as influential, if not more influential, than payment companies are today. And they would almost certainly become the orchestrators of important new ecosystems.

Some ecosystem businesses may even opt to build more offline capabilities—wagering that the safety of being unhackable is worth the downside of reduced connectivity. This could lead to break-throughs in advanced technologies for secure communication, like so-called quantum entanglement communications, which some technologists contend could allow for unhackable, faster-than-light transmissions.[21] All in all, in the scenario of such an extreme cyber event, we would be likely to see the ecosystem economy turned inside out by major changes in the cybersecurity landscape.

ACCELERATION OF SPACE-BASED COMMERCE

At present, there are numerous obstacles that make large-scale eco-nomic activity in outer-space impossible—most notably, the high cost of launching and retrieving rockets. But this hasn't deterred a throng of eager investors and entrepreneurs from putting energy into solving those problems—and dreaming big about the transformative possibili-ties of bringing commerce to space. According to a recent analysis by Morgan Stanley, the global space industry could be generating as much a $1 trillion in revenue by 2040.[22]

But as with technological developments such as artificial intelli-gence, it's possible that we will see a rapid, previously inconceivable acceleration in technological progress that will change our sense of what's possible in space. As the Morgan Stanley report pointed out, "A single transformative technology shift often can spark new eras of modernization, followed by a flurry of complimentary innovations."[23] Perhaps scientists will invent a new kind of propulsion system, or hap-pen upon a technological or chemical breakthrough that makes the process of launching objects into space much cheaper and much more convenient. Or perhaps they will find a way to recover and reuse rock-ets more effectively and efficiently than is possible today.

The implications for ecosystems would be enormous. There is already a nascent micro-ecosystem developing around space-based commerce. But as a report from the *Harvard Business Review* pointed out, thus far, economic activity in space has been confined mostly to areas that probably seem rather ordinary to us today. This is what's called the space-for-earth economy—"that is, goods or services produced in space for use on earth . . . [including] telecommunications and internet infrastructure, earth observation capabilities, national security satellites, and more."[24] However, in the event of a sudden acceleration, we could see a much broader and stronger ecosystem form around space-related activities and commerce, which would include asteroid mining, large-scale space tourism, and much more. This is certainly an area where ecosystems could be transformative since some of the individual businesses within it would need to cross-finance others. Even with rapid advances in technology that lower the cost of sending people and materials into space, that task will likely continue to be the most expensive part of the proposition. In order to make it worthwhile, therefore, the companies that manage and plan rocket launches (or whatever new technology takes their place) will need to partner with other businesses that can deliver more value. All of this would spur the creation of numerous micro-ecosystems within the larger, dynamic space ecosystem.

One such micro-ecosystem could form around asteroid mining, which stands to change the mineral economy throughout the world for hundreds of years to come. With the right advancements in spaceflight technology, and the right allocation of resources, it's conceivable that a company could bring mining equipment to a passing asteroid in order to extract whatever valuable deposits it may contain—from basic materials like iron to precious metals like platinum. As Martin Elvis of Harvard University's Center for Astrophysics writes, "Being an idealistic astrophysicist, my interest is in the money to be made from [asteroids]. That really is idealistic because, if we can make a profit mining the asteroids, then doing bigger things in space will become a lot cheaper."[25] For this reason, even with a major technological breakthrough, the rise of a space ecosystem is likely to be fueled in large part by immediately profitable enterprises like asteroid mining.

An acceleration of space technology is also likely to give a significant boost to several existing ecosystems. A wide array of new possibilities would be opened up in the mobility ecosystem; for example, traffic between earth and space increases and new sources of energy are needed to fuel that travel. According to a report from the World Economic Forum, two potential sources for this energy, which are likely to be the basis of important ecosystem activity, are chemical rockets and solar energy, which is "more effective when gathered in space due to the lack of a filtering atmosphere."[26]

BIOTECHNOLOGY

Accelerations in other areas of technology could also have a significant impact on how certain ecosystems develop, and what they will be focused on. One area that could play a particularly important role is biotechnology. In recent decades, scientists have made previously unimaginable strides toward developing biotechnologies capable of extending the human lifespan, curing diseases like cancer, and solving an array of confounding societal problems.

One of the most promising of these technologies is CRISPR, a tool for locating and editing a specific bit of DNA inside a cell. The name is an acronym for "clustered regularly interspaced short palindromic repeats," a reference to the pattern created in DNA by the protein that the technology relies on, which is called Cas.[27] CRISPR can be used to modify the genomes of plants and animals and to treat or prevent many diseases.[28] In the future, tools like CRISPR will allow scientists and doctors to quickly analyze genetic materials, enabling them not only to develop sophisticated personalized medicines but also to combat diseases that today seem intractable—and rapidly develop vaccines to guard against emerging pathogens.

Scientists have made preliminary advances that show the potential for one day using CRISPR-enabled gene editing to slow down the aging process and extend the human lifespan. According to a professor of bioengineering at Stanford University, Dr. Lei Stanely Qi, "As we learn how to use CRISPR-Cas to study DNA as a system, it becomes possible to imagine one day developing safe techniques to treat many adverse consequences of aging."[29]

Another area that shows great promise and carries potentially transformative implications is biocomputing, or the use of biological materials for computing purposes. According to a recent McKinsey report, "Potential is growing for interfaces between biological systems and computers. . . . Biocomputers that use biology to mimic silicon are being researched, including the use of DNA to store data. DNA is about one million times denser than hard-disk storage; technically, one kilogram of raw DNA could store the entirety of the world's data."[30]

Other applications of biotechnology could help solve other pressing concerns for humanity. CRISPR-enabled gene editing, for example, could be used to modify cattle to produce smaller quantities of greenhouse gases like methane, a significant contributor to global warming.[31]

Gene editing could also be used to engineer new crops perfectly suited to use in biofuels, helping to create a cheaper, more sustainable energy source. Or it could potentially be used to engineer bacteria or other microorganisms to aid in capturing carbon emissions.

Even if these technologies continue on their present trajectory, they will still have a huge impact on the global economy. But as with artificial intelligence and other technologies we have considered, we can also imagine a world in which there is a dramatic acceleration in how quickly they are developed and deployed.

The effects of such an acceleration would be staggering—particularly on the development of ecosystems. With diseases like cancer vanquished, and the human lifespan significantly extended, we would need to make some important changes to the way we organize our lives and our economic activity. The elderly are already projected to become a much larger portion of the global population, but with a big leap forward in life-extending biotechnologies, they could become an even bigger segment of the population. This would have all sorts of implications. For example, with longer lifespans, humans would likely need more artificial implants, prosthetics, and other components to maintain their quality of life further and further into old age—which would potentially lead to significant growth and expansion of the elder care micro-ecosystem. Health care, nursing homes, assisted-care, and insurance would all be significantly impacted. There would also be enormous effects within the wealth and protection ecosystem as longer lifespans change the way that people think about retirement and savings.

Other developments would affect an even broader range of ecosystems. Biocomputing, for example, could have the general effect of boosting all ecosystems by drastically reducing the cost of computing power. CRISPR-enabled modification of plants and animals could give a huge boost to the climate-change–focused micro-ecosystems we discussed earlier.

NANOTECHNOLOGY

One of the most extreme drivers of ecosystem growth that we can imagine is the possibility of a breakthrough in nanotechnology, or the manipulation of matter on a microscopic level. In the past, nanotech has frequently been cited as a speculative game-changing technology of the distant future—a kind of technology that might become indistinguishable from magic. And while some of the most dramatic potential applications remain beyond our reach, there are many brilliant, hardworking researchers today laying the groundwork for such miracles. In recent years, for example, scientists have made astounding strides in the development of graphene, a new carbon-based material. According to researchers at Carnegie Mellon University, the material is composed of "a single layer of carbon atoms connected in a hexagonal pattern" and is "nearly 200 times stronger than steel, flexible, nearly transparent, and highly conductive to heat and electricity."[32] At the same time, new and even more consequential breakthroughs may loom in the future.

If and when such a breakthrough happens, the impact will be intense and wide-ranging. There would be applications in medicine, in computing, in construction, in environmental preservation—and many other areas. In medicine, microscopically small sensors could enable doctors to monitor patients' vital signs with far greater precision than is possible now. As Professor of Nanotechnology at the University of Southampton Themis Prodromakis writes, "we could go further by implanting or injecting tiny sensors inside our bodies. This would capture much more detailed information with less hassle to the patient, enabling doctors to personalise their treatment."[33] Eventually, it's even possible that artificially-engineered organisms, or robots, on a nanoscale could be used to enter the body and address problems with extreme precision.[34] There are exciting possibilities in engineering and construction, as well. As Professor Prodromakis continues, "Changing the structure of materials at the nanoscale can give them some amazing properties—by giving them a texture that repels water, for example. In the future, nanotechnology coatings or additives will even have the potential to allow materials to 'heal' when damaged or worn. For example, dispersing nanoparticles throughout a material means that they can migrate to fill in any cracks that appear."

All of these changes and advances would, of course, have a profound effect on ecosystems. Imagine the incredible value propositions that ecosystem players would be able to design around, say, personalized medicine with nanotechnology at their disposal. The health ecosystem would potentially see a frenzy of activity as companies scramble to design new comprehensive, end-to-end patient journeys based on the new technology. As would other ecosystems like mobility, housing, and public services.

But perhaps the biggest potential impact of nanotechnology on ecosystems would be that it would extend their reach beyond just distribution, to manufacturing as well. Recall that with the rise of globalization toward the end of the twentieth century, we saw a decline in manufacturing in the Western world. Nanotechnology may be the catalyst that brings manufacturing back to the West, driving the creation of a whole new collection of macro- and micro-ecosystems.

With sufficient progress in the field of nanotechnology, we may be able to manipulate matter on an atomic level with sufficient detail that products would be able to be printed in consumers' homes or at the point of sale—rather than being manufactured in a low-wage country and then shipped overseas. This sort of technology, orders of magnitude more sophisticated than current 3D printing technology, would stand to completely upend the consumer marketplace ecosystem. Imagine being able to order a desk, or a notebook, or a chair, or an umbrella—and have it built in front of you, atom by atom, as you wait. There would also be transformative applications in the construction sector. Imagine—instead of building a house, brick by brick, you could simply command a fleet of microscopic robots to grow a house.

The implications of this are significant. Thus far ecosystems have been largely focused on services rather than manufacturing. But with a major acceleration of scientific progress, nanotechnology-driven manufacturing could become incorporated into ecosystems. In the shelter/home ecosystem, for example, we can imagine a service that would fulfill traditional housing needs like finding and buying real estate, purchasing insurance, and getting a mortgage—but would also allow you to have your house built on-demand by a fleet of nanobots.

Soon, we would see the emergence of a huge new manufacturing ecosystem, driven largely by nanotech players. The effects of this ecosystem would be striking. Because nanotechnology would be capable of quickly and efficiently fabricating almost any item, the ownership of physical objects would become far less important while design would become far more important. This would amount to a complete restructuring of the way we, as a society, think about property and value.

All of this may sound a bit far-fetched, but it is all firmly within the realm of possibility. Before long, it will simply not be an option for businesses to continue on without thinking more carefully and proactively about how the evolution of ecosystems will affect them. Even for some companies that thus far have managed to avoid the upheavals of the ecosystem revolution, staying on the same course may no longer be possible. But at the same time, emerging technologies will open huge opportunities—not only for making a profit and building successful businesses, but for improving the well-being of humanity and helping us to survive a series of existential threats.

The forces driving the evolution of ecosystems may also come as a complete surprise. We have laid out in this chapter a number of different forces that we think will play important roles in shaping their trajectory, but there will surely be many others, some of which are beyond our power to imagine at present. Take the COVID-19 pandemic of the early 2020s. That illness, and the wave of different policies adopted around the globe to combat it, had a remarkable effect on the development of ecosystems, accelerating digital adoption and permanently normalizing certain consumer behaviors like curbside pickup. We certainly hope that the unseen forces that await us in the future will not cause nearly so much pain and suffering as the COVID pandemic, but there is truly no telling what lies in store. Before 2020 would any of us have predicted such a momentous event as the COVID pandemic?

In the first three chapters of this book, we have covered the past, present, and future of ecosystems. We have examined the reasons for their emergence, the effects of the transformation they have precipitated, and their continued trajectory. For the practically-minded, this leaves an enormous, glaring question: What should we do about all of this? How should we navigate this new world of ecosystems? This will be the subject of the second part of this book. Now that we understand how ecosystems work, and how they might emerge and evolve, we are ready to wade into the thorny matter of how we can adapt to the changing environment.

Part Two

4

Going Where the Puck Will Be

Choosing Where to Play in the New Ecosystem Economy

In every learning experience, there comes a point when it's time to put theory into action—to take the abstract principles you've absorbed and apply them in the real world. This is the point we've now reached. In Part One of this book, we told the story of how ecosystems are transforming our economy—taking you through their past, present, and future. Now it's time to think about what that future holds for you, the reader—presumably someone who has a stake in the progress of the economy, someone who is interested in growing a business and having a broader positive impact on society. In Part Two, we will consider the implications of the ecosystem economy, and enumerate some steps you can take to give yourself the best possible shot at success.

As we move into a more practical discussion of ecosystems, it's good to remind ourselves of what exactly we mean when we use that word. Ecosystems, you'll recall, are communities of interconnected digital and physical businesses that work across the boundaries between traditional sectors of the economy to provide what customers need. Businesses form ecosystems by partnering with one another—by sharing assets, information, and resources—and ultimately creating value beyond what would have been possible for each of them to achieve individually. Ecosystems, we should remember, are distinct from traditional partnerships among businesses like vendor and customer relationships. A vendor agrees to supply something to a customer and gets paid in return. In a typical ecosystem relationship, by contrast, multiple businesses collectively provide products or services to meet customers' needs and share the value they have created in the process. As you begin to think practically about how you might adapt to this emerging ecosystem economy, it's important to keep in mind this basic sense of what makes ecosystems so special and powerful.

This power can present differently to different people. Some will fixate on the daunting challenges it could pose, while others will focus on its potential to bring enormous wealth and success—and to effect a positive impact on society. As Napoleon Bonaparte famously remarked, "There are only two forces that unite men—fear and interest." The French emperor clearly favored the former—he finished the thought by saying, "All great revolutions originate in fear, for the play of interests does not lead to accomplishment."[1] In the business world today, we tend to think that most important decisions are driven by a combination of the two. Whether you find fear or interest the more compelling message, it is probably the case that both will drive your thinking—and anyway, what is essential is that you heed their message. It doesn't matter whether you're motivated by the huge potential rewards of the ecosystem economy and the opportunity to make a positive change in society—or by fear of being made irrelevant. What matters is that you need to act.

As you start adapting to the new ecosystem economy, the first questions you need to answer are: Where will you compete now? And what should you do to evolve your value proposition? These are difficult, thorny questions, and it's only natural to struggle with them. In this chapter, we will lay out for you a thoughtful, deliberative, and powerful process for finding answers to these questions. The steps we have devised include some measures you may already be taking—and some that will be new.

Of course, every company is already engaged in some manner of strategic planning. We are not proposing that you completely replace that. But what we are saying is that you will need to vastly expand your scope—and shift the nature of your planning. Doing so may push your thinking in ways that run counter to what your routine strategic planning is telling you—and you need to be prepared to wrestle with this tension. For instance, to survive in the evolving ecosystem economy, most companies will need to significantly alter their business models, which will inevitably involve painful sacrifices in the short term. You may have to cannibalize existing businesses to lay the groundwork for a future ecosystem play. Especially if the proposition you want to offer necessitates creating a new ecosystem or building a new platform, you may need to offer some services for free—and eat the associated costs.

As challenging as this new type of planning may be in the short term, it does not end there. Rather, this process needs to be constantly maintained and reassessed. Many successful ecosystem businesses got ahead not because they started with a master plan and flawlessly executed it exactly as originally conceived—rather, they succeeded thanks to their adaptability, their knack for recognizing shifting circumstances and course-correcting. A few other characteristics of successful ecosystem businesses include embracing an agile, adaptable mindset in order to compete in a highly dynamic world where customer needs and technology are taking unpredictable twists and turns. Later in this book, in Chapter 6, we will cover how an agile mindset and approach will help you adapt to the new ecosystem economy. In a sense, what we're saying is that you will be best positioned to take advantage of the effects of the ecosystem economy if you know which direction you want to go with your ecosystem business and adopt a mindset that allows for making adjustments as you go.

So many companies understand that they need to evolve their propositions but underestimate the scale at which change is needed. To do so effectively, you need to think backward from the future, not forward from the present—but this does not necessarily mean that you need to emulate tech companies or try to envision what amazing futuristic technologies we will have in 50 years. Instead, you need to fundamentally rethink how you define your customers' needs, your customer base, your industry, your proposition, and the competitive landscape.

Again, we start by choosing where to play, and how to evolve your proposition. The process we've designed will help you on both fronts. It includes four main steps, which we'll lay out for you here before explaining them in more detail through the lens of several examples.

1. **Start with the Basics**: The first step is to go back to the basics and adopt a customer-centric view. Clearly define for yourself what value propositions you are currently offering your customers. How are those propositions meeting customers' current needs? Can you continue to meet your customers' needs as those needs change and as your customer base itself changes—especially in the context of the two big trends we described earlier: technological development and changes in consumer behavior? How can you evolve your propositions to meet customers' needs in the future—before they are even aware of the need? We can break these questions down into several key areas:

   a. **Assessment of customer needs and customer base:** How are your customers' needs, preferences, and consumption patterns going to change in the future as technology evolves and other trends progress? Think about this not just in terms of your current sector or industry—but rather, consider the influence that other industries and sectors will exert on your sector and how they will shape your customers' needs. Similarly, ask yourself how your customer base itself may change over time, in response to those trends—will it expand? Shrink? Shift? Will you attract an entirely new kind of customer? How can you anticipate customer needs before your customers even recognize them as such? As you think through these questions, remember to always take a cross-sectoral view.

   b. **Propositions:** Based on the answers to the preceding questions about your customers' needs and your customer base, ask yourself: How should you evolve the proposition you are offering customers to better meet their needs both now and in the future? In other words, how should you evolve your customer offers? Again, it is essential to break out of the provincialism of your own sector or industry and adopt a cross-sectoral view. Ask yourself: Where do you have opportunities to make differentiated offers and propositions—not just for customers within your current sector, but also for your potentially expanding customer base?

   c. **Differentiated bets:** Consider the different propositions you have generated in step 1b, and prioritize them based on where you might have a differentiated advantage. What differentiated bets are you going to make to meet the needs of your customers with your propositions? This will naturally define where you should play going forward.

2. **Ecosystem Assessment:** To successfully carry out the new proposition that you defined in step 1, you need to undertake a comprehensive ecosystem assessment—in other words, you need to identify where there is an opportunity for such a proposition to thrive. The ecosystem assessment consists of two important parts:

   a. **The current situation:** Taking into consideration your evolving customer base, your customers' evolving needs, and your differentiated bets, ask yourself: Do I need an ecosystem to pull off the proposition? (If the answer is no, perhaps you are not being ambitious enough with your proposition—perhaps you should dream bigger.) Then ask: Are there any currently existing ecosystems out there that could meet your customers' evolving needs? If yes, what are they? And what are their strengths and weaknesses? How might these ecosystems evolve in the future? Is it possible for you to leverage these ecosystems or co-exist with them? Or will you have to compete with them?

   b. **Finding gaps:** If the answer is no—if there aren't currently any ecosystems capable of meeting the evolving needs of your evolving customer base—then you need to ask: What ecosystems are needed? What is the gap a new ecosystem could fill?

3. **Competitive Assessment:** With your new proposition defined, and the ecosystem opportunity identified, you now need to assess the competition. Ask yourself: Given the acceleration of technological developments, consumer behavior trends, evolving customer needs, and the ecosystem landscape, what sort of competition can you expect in the future—both within your own sector and from beyond? You can divide this step into three sub-parts:

   a. **Traditional competitors:** Who are your traditional competitors—or the players you have competed with historically? What are their strengths and weaknesses? How might they evolve to meet emerging customer needs and an evolving customer base? Are they evolving into potential partners or collaborators?

   b. **New competitors:** Who are your emerging ecosystem-based competitors? In other words, which competitors haven't yet been in the space much—if at all—but are beginning to lever-age some of the emerging technology and consumer trends we identified above? What are these competitors' strengths and weaknesses? And how might they evolve to meet emerging customer needs and a changing customer base?

c. **Competitive stance:** What is your position relative to these competitors—especially the emerging ecosystem competitors? What ground can you stake out that will enable you to carry out your value proposition and remain more attractive than your ecosystem competitors?

4. **Repeat the Cycle:** Finally, the last step is to repeat the first three—both to be sure you're choosing the right path in the present moment, and to ensure that you remain flexible and attuned to changing circumstances going forward. First, repeat the process a few times, refining or adjusting your first-cut answers to be sure they are sound and actionable. Then, even after you have formed a concrete plan and begun to act on it, come back and revisit these steps every few quarters to ensure that your answer still makes sense as the landscape shifts. Figure 4.1 illustrates this perpetual reassessment. As you come

FIGURE 4.1   **An approach to determine where to play in the new ecosystem economy**

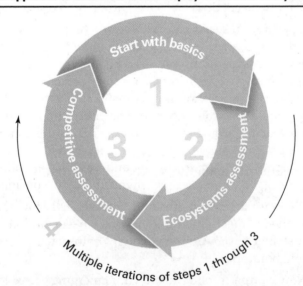

back to these steps, you may also find it helpful to use some more focused exercises and simulations, like war-gaming and red-teaming (both of which we'll cover later in the chapter).

By the end of this process, you should have a much stronger sense of where you are ideally suited to play—and a robust portfolio of ideas for evolving your value proposition to meet the changing times. However, thus far, our discussion of this process has been a bit theoretical. To show how it works in more practical terms, we'll now explain it by way of a few examples.

EXAMPLE 1: MOBILITY AS A SERVICE

Imagine you are a player in the current automotive sector. Exactly what kind of player isn't important—and in fact, for the sake of discussion, let's imagine that you are a somewhat generic player. You could be, for instance, an original equipment manufacturer (OEM) in the automotive space, a company that makes software for cars, a component supplier, a sub-systems supplier to the automotive industry, or a cloud player or other technology player trying to make an autonomous driving play. Regardless of what sort of player you are, it's likely that you will need to reassess where you play in light of the new ecosystem economy. If that's the case, let us imagine how you might go through our process.

Step 1a: Assessment of customer needs and customer base

The process begins with an assessment of how your customers' needs are evolving and how your customer base may be changing. As the superstar hockey player Wayne Gretzky once famously said, "I skate to where the puck is going to be, not where it has been."[2] Similarly, we need to anticipate how our customers and their needs will shift over time, and work proactively to meet them. To begin, consider the two main drivers of ecosystem growth that we explored back in Chapter 2: an accelerating pace of technological progress and evolving consumer behaviors and expectations. How do these trends intersect with the traditional automotive sector? Sensor technology, Lidar, cameras, artificial intelligence, machine learning, and other capabilities have all advanced significantly in recent years. Together, these advancements are helping to make semi- and fully-autonomous vehicles a reality in the near future.[3] The technology for electric vehicles (EVs) is already quite developed and only getting better.[4] Advancements in AR and VR technology, meanwhile, are opening new possibilities for highly inter-active interfaces and entertainment within cars. Already today there is so much technology getting packed into cars that some have called them "data centers on wheels"—and this will only increase in the future.[5]

At the same time, consumers are changing their behaviors—driven in large part by the convenience of new technologies and new inte-grated propositions. For example, as app-based ridesharing and food- or package-delivery services become more ubiquitous, consumers are becoming accustomed to having a significant portion of their needs ful-filled by "as a service"–model offerings. Conditioned by players like Amazon and others, consumers are more and more coming to expect any provider of products or services to essentially read their minds and proactively fulfill their needs. We don't see any reason why consumers wouldn't have a similar expectation when it come to their mobility needs.

So what does this mean for you, our example automotive player? As these trends build, how are your customers' needs changing? And how is your customer base evolving? To find the answers to these questions, let's think through the implications of the technology and consumer trends we just covered. Together, these changes will amount to a shift in how cars fit into society. Today, we think of a car as a machine that is usually owned by individuals for getting from point A to point B. But in the near- to medium-term future, we may come to see them more as liminal spaces that are used and paid for on-demand while moving between locations. In other words, we may come to see them as living rooms on wheels or offices on wheels.[6] Consider, for example, how the interior of a car would be transformed when we have the technology to support fully autonomous vehicles—without the need for steering wheels, gas and brake pedals, a dashboard, or many other components of a car's interior that seem essential today, a great deal of space would be freed up for other uses. The entire design of the car's interior could be reimagined.

The reverberations of such a shift would be profound: individual car ownership could decrease dramatically. Instead, companies may own a much larger portion of the cars on the road at any given time. In turn, the way cars are designed and sold would change as well. Fewer cars would be needed overall because the companies that own or man-age them would, in all likelihood, use them much more efficiently than individually-owned cars are used today. By some estimations, the average car today sits unused for 95 percent of its life.[7] With the arrival of fully autonomous cars, and with sophisticated algorithms for managing how they are scheduled and routed, the companies that own or operate these cars would be able to keep them in use for a much larger portion of the time.

In turn, many functions and sub-sectors within the traditional automotive sector would be transformed—and this is where we begin to see the shifting customer needs and customer base. Imagine, for instance, that you are a financial services player in the automotive space. With far fewer individually owned cars, there would be less of a need for consumer car loans than there is today—your customer base would shrink. At the same time, you may find new takers for your offering—for instance, you might pivot to financing cars for rideshare players or other participants in an emerging mobility ecosystem. Moving to a slightly different example, imagine that you are an automotive dealership—with far fewer individual customers interested in buying cars, there may not be a need for you anymore—at least in the form that you exist today. You may find that you are no longer selling to individuals, but instead to asset owners, like financial players that buy or finance cars for other business, such as ridesharing platforms or autonomous car services. Similarly, car repair networks would need to be significantly retooled as fewer and fewer consumers would have personally owned cars to bring in for repair. So would retail auto shops that sell parts and accessories to consumers.

However, not every player would find their customer base shifting in a negative way. As consumers get more and more comfortable using autonomous vehicle mobility services, those players may end up expanding their customer base in some unexpected ways. At present, automotive consumers are limited by age. A driver's license is needed to operate a vehicle, and licenses are available only to people older than 16 in the US or 18 in many other places. But autonomous vehicles could remove this limitation. There is no reason a person younger than 18 or even 16 wouldn't be able to use an autonomous vehicle mobility service—with parental permission, if applicable, of course. Furthermore, with an autonomous vehicle service (powered partly by advanced connectivity and app-based capabilities with precision mapping) you would not only be serving customers in the traditional auto sector but also customers in other sectors like logistics—with services that are already prevalent like package delivery and food delivery. Automotive players with the vision to plan for these changes could see their customer base extended to entirely new groups.

It's important to distinguish here how the goals of step 1a are different from the ordinary sort of planning that companies are already engaged in. With our approach, you are breaking out of a sector-based view of customers. So many of the customer analyses and projections that companies are doing now are strongly shaped by the traditional sectors in which they operate. Customer surveys, for example, will ask questions about different brands and products within a single sector. Instead, you need to seek a much broader understanding of your customers: not only their preferences, but their behaviors and attitudes—and not only within your sector, but across many sectors. You need to get an all-encompassing, panoramic view of their economic life.

By the end of step 1a, you will hopefully have gained a deeper understanding of the underlying dynamics that will shape your current propositions in the future—and this will give you the grounding you need to begin thinking about evolving your proposition in step 1b.

Step 1b: Propositions

After considering your changing customer base and their evolving needs, we continue our process by assessing the propositions you are currently offering and determining how to evolve them given the insights we gained from step 1a. If you are an automotive OEM, for instance, your proposition has traditionally been manufacturing cars and selling them (often through intermediaries) to both consumers and businesses. In the new ecosystem world, you need to find a way of shifting or growing that proposition. There are a multitude of options. To take just one example, you could enter into the proposition of offering mobility as a service by owning (and potentially operating) the cars you produce in a semi-vertically-integrated fashion. By mobility as a service, we mean an on-demand, app-based service that allows users to request and get picked up by an autonomous vehicle, which would then deliver them to their chosen destination for a price to be determined by mileage, demand, and other factors.

Alternatively, you could choose a narrower focus that is still attuned to the big technology and consumer shifts you have observed. You could, for instance, concentrate on building cars designed to be integrated into a living-room-on-wheels or office-on-wheels proposition—that is to say, you could center your business on turning cars into comfortable, luxury spaces to be rented while moving between locations. While this is an attractive proposition, pursuing it would mean completely changing how you think about your core product. In the future, if it's true that fewer cars will be necessary, their design would need to be completely overhauled to accommodate the new role that cars would play in society. As we mentioned earlier, in such a scenario, it's likely that autonomous cars would be deployed much more efficiently than individually owned cars are today. As such, they would need to be designed to be kept running for a much greater portion of each day. They would also need to be more spacious and equipped with better amenities to meet rising consumer expectations. Fortunately, these cars would require neither a driver nor an internal combustion engine, meaning there would be significantly more room on board for the furniture and equipment necessary to create the desired space—whether a living room, office, or some other room-on-wheels.

For other players in the automotive space, the process of assessing and evolving your propositions may look a little different. If you are a software component or systems player in the auto industry, for instance, you could offer a software platform that serves as a sort of operating system for mobility-as-service players, including all the many capabilities that come with connected and intelligent cars. If you're a manufacturer of car seats, you might pivot to making other sorts of furniture for cars—pieces that are more comfortable or better suited to the living-room-on-wheels proposition.

Again, we might ask: How is step 1b any different from what companies are currently doing and planning? Of course, thinking about how to refine your value proposition is not a radical idea, but we are proposing something more than that. You need to not only push the proposition forward, but completely reinvent it. You might, for example, convene a planning session where the goal is to completely forget what you do today—to imagine you are investing anew with a blank slate. Rather than working forward from your current position, work backward from a position of having the freedom to do anything. Bring people from outside your industry into the conversation as well. Only if you are able to think with freshness and vitality will you be able to create propositions that will succeed in a world of sectors without borders.

Step 1c: Differentiated bets

By the time you are finished with step 1b, you should have a portfolio of at least a half-dozen different options for evolving your proposition in response to your changing customer needs and a changing customer base. However, it's simply not possible to pursue every one of these ideas. In step 1c, therefore, we narrow these options down, and prioritize them based on where we might have differentiated capabilities or some other special advantage (either now or in the future).

There are a number of different areas where you might hold such an advantage. One is data. If you have collected or obtained exclusive access to some especially illuminating set of data—whether about your customers, your competitors, the market, or something else—this could be a powerful advantage that you can use to distinguish your proposition. Another potential advantage you might have is a first-mover advantage—obviously, if you are the first out of the gate, you will enjoy a head start over your rivals, especially if you can achieve a so-called network effect. Another advantage might be pre-existing customer relationships—if people are familiar with your business and trust you because of products or services you've provided in another sector, you will have an edge over other players in attracting them to your proposition. When you take all of these factors together, chances are that they will go a long way toward showing you which of the propositions on your list you have the best chance of succeeding with.

Let us explore a few examples to show how this process of prioritization might work. If you are, say, an automotive OEM focused on EVs, and you have been experimenting with autonomous cars, it is likely that you will have gathered a valuable set of data from that experimentation—data that others would likely not have access to.[8] If indeed you are the only one with access to this data set, it could end up being a big differentiator as you seek to make a mobility-as-a-service play. If you are, say, a cloud player that has been experimenting with autonomous vehicle mobility by partnering with a variety of different OEMs, you too will have somewhat of a data advantage to make a differentiated bet either on your own or in ecosystem partnership with others.[9] This data advantage, however, may prove to be short lived—since other companies that enter the space later will collect their own data, and eventually catch up. It is also possible that regulation around data will negate the advantage—if, as we discussed in Chapter 3, governments start requiring companies to share their data via open APIs.

Of course, this process of prioritization may bear some resemblance to the way that many companies today evaluate and choose between different potential value propositions. What distinguishes our process are the parameters that you use to make the determination. When you are considering where you may have a differentiated advantage, what ultimately drives your thinking should be cross-sectoral opportunities. In narrowing down your options in search of the strongest ecosystem-based proposition, you will naturally gravitate toward those propositions that create value by crossing sector borders to cooperatively fulfill customer needs. We believe that building an ecosystem backbone will create a protective moat around your propositions and help you to deliver value for all the key stakeholders involved.

To summarize, step 1 is about taking a close look at your customers, and letting their changing needs and priorities guide your path. By the time you are finished with this step, you should have a handful of solid options for different ways to evolve your proposition, each of which is attuned not only to your differentiated advantages and capabilities—but also to your shifting customer base and the shifting ecosystem landscape.

Step 2a: The current situation

Step 2 of our process, you will recall, is a comprehensive ecosystem assessment, the goal of which is to identify an opportunity that is ripe for an ecosystem solution. Now that you have a sense of your evolving customer base and your customers' evolving needs, ask yourself: Are there any currently existing ecosystems that could meet those needs? If so, what are they? And what are their strengths and weaknesses? How might these ecosystems evolve in the future? Continuing with the automotive example previously described, suppose you are an OEM wanting to make a mobility-as-a-service offer in the new evolving ecosystem economy. Start by considering your immediate surroundings—the players you already do business with. You may not be part of a true ecosystem yet, but it's likely that you do have numerous supplier- or vendor-customer relationships with various players in the industry, and some of these players could end up fulfilling a role in an ecosystem if you were to create one. Consider a software platform vendor you already do business with, like an infotainment supplier that supplies platform software to entertain consumers in the car. This player could end up being a valuable partner in a mobility-as-a-service ecosystem.

Similarly, current rideshare platform players like Uber and Lyft might end up being part of the ecosystem. These rideshare platforms already have their own healthy ecosystems in place—ecosystems that connect drivers and car owners with consumers via an app to provide mobility as a service. Because of this, these rideshare platforms would already have robust networks of drivers to draw from as well as strong pre-existing customer relationships. The combined effect would be a strong first-mover advantage. How might these existing ecosystems evolve in the future? The current, platform-based rideshare ecosystem players are developing in at least two different directions. One direction involves offering mobility as a service for food- and package-delivery services. The other involves transitioning from driver-based shared mobility to autonomous vehicle-based shared mobility.

As ecosystems continue to emerge, however, we may begin to see a wider variety of different kinds of business models developing—and to stay competitive, it will be necessary to anticipate this evolution. For instance, rideshare players currently operate by charging customers at a variable rate based on distance, demand, and other factors. But in the future, that calculation may change. It may be, for example, that companies find a way to charge less by offsetting the expense of the ride—by introducing an advertising component, or by deriving valuable data. As you assess the ecosystem landscape, you need to not only evaluate ecosystems as they are now, but to take into account how their business models may shift over time in response to ongoing trends.

Step 2b: Finding gaps

Next, given what you determined about your customers' evolving needs, your evolving customer base, and the propositions you developed to deliver distinct value by making an ecosystem play, ask yourself: What ecosystem gaps do you need to fill? Some players that want to take advantage of shifting tech and consumer trends to create an ecosystem may find that there are no currently existing ecosystems capable of meeting customers' evolving needs—that their own traditional vendor-customer relationships are insufficient, as are other existing ecosystems. If this is true—if there aren't currently any ecosystems capable of fully meeting the evolving needs of an evolving customer base—then ask yourself: What ecosystems are needed? Let us return to the example of a financial player or investor in the automotive space looking to make a mobility-as-a-service play by leveraging autonomous vehicles. Today, this player may be a vendor providing auto financing to OEMs or dealers. If this player wanted to transition to a mobility-as-a-service offer, and determined that its current ecosystem is not up to the task, it would need to either figure out how to work within existing ecosystems to augment its capabilities—or pull together an entirely new ecosystem. Such an ecosystem would need a shared-mobility or rideshare software platform provider, an OEM to supply cars, and some other entity to maintain and service the cars, among others.

Or take another example. This time, let's suppose you are a component supplier or sub-system player also wanting to make—or at least participate in—a mobility-as-a-service play. Again, you would likely find yourself with only part of the ecosystem you need to pull it off. You would have to either pull together a new ecosystem (which could be quite challenging given your starting position) or transform your current proposition into one more compatible with mobility as a service. The same would be true for a content or media player, which could offer compelling entertainment or business content to make the living room, office room or entertainment room more attractive for users. In each of these examples, along with the capabilities you already bring to the table, you would also need an online or software player that could combine and coordinate your capabilities through an app-based rideshare platform for consumers.

In any case, when you are choosing whether to develop a new ecosystem or work within an existing ecosystem, a significant part of your decision consists of determining what role you should play—that is to say, determining whether your natural position is as an ecosystem orchestrator or as a participant. This matter of determining your role will be the focus of the next chapter.

Once again, we want to be very clear about how step 2 of our process, the ecosystem assessment, differs from the traditional planning that companies typically engage in. It is quite common for companies today to look for a gap that they can use to successfully execute their proposition. But the difference here is that we are looking for an *ecosystem* gap—in other words, we are looking for a gap that can only be filled by an integrated offering that incorporates elements from multiple different sectors. Most companies today are still approaching this task from a vendor/supplier-customer view. What they need is an ecosystem-based approach. Another difference is that we are adopting a future-back perspective instead of a present-forward perspective. Rather than extrapolating what the needs for different ecosystems may be in the future, we are imagining an exciting future scenario in which a particular set of customer needs are effectively and efficiently fulfilled—and then working backward to determine which ecosystems are needed to get there. In other words, which ecosystem gaps exist that need to be addressed?

After you finish your assessment of existing ecosystems and determine the need for new ecosystems to pull off the proposition, it is time to start putting a stake in the ground. Do you want to leverage existing ecosystems? Modify an existing ecosystem? Or do you need to build an entirely new ecosystem? Keep in mind that building a new ecosystem from scratch can be a daunting task. If you are modifying an existing ecosystem, which existing players do you want to leverage? And which ones would you prefer to outcompete? If you are building a new ecosystem, who are the new players you will need to build it? In other words, step 2 is all about assessing the ecosystem landscape—now it is time to chart your path through that landscape.

Step 3a: Traditional competitors

The third step of our process, we will recall, is a competitive assessment. As we have seen, in the future, technology and consumer changes will remake the world around us. You will need to assess how your customer needs and customer base are changing, weigh different options for evolving your proposition, and assemble a new set of cross-sectoral capabilities to execute your play. But this is just one side of the equation. At the same time, you will face an entirely new set of competitors. Who will they be? In the old world of sectors, it was easy to tell: your competitors were your neighbors, the other players operating within your sector. But in the ecosystem economy, with increasingly porous borders between sectors, it will be difficult to predict where competition will come from. Those who were once your partners or collaborators may now turn out to be competitors. And those who were once fierce competitors may now turn out to be allies. What is critical is getting a sense of how the lines have shifted and sizing up other players as quickly and accurately as possible.

Taking into account the many shifting factors we have already explored—tech changes, consumer changes, your customers' evolving needs, and the ecosystem landscape—we will try to assess what sort of competition we can expect in the future. As we do this, we must always remember that in the ecosystem economy, competition can come from any direction—not just from within our own sector, but from any player capable of making a cross-sector play.

In the first part of this step, 3a, we begin by assessing your traditional competitors—or in other words, the players you have competed with historically. What are their strengths and weaknesses? How might they evolve to meet emerging customer needs and an evolving customer base? Are they likely to evolve in ways similar to what you are planning? Ecosystems are likely to both motivate and enable traditional competitors to leapfrog you. The pressures on margins and market share from new entrants can strongly incentivize weaker, smaller players to take big risks with new business models—for example, by partnering with an outside attacker. In such an environment, a business absolutely must expect and prepare for surprises. For example, war-gaming—a process of simulating and preparing for certain scenarios and outcomes—may be a useful exercise (we will cover its potential uses in more detail later in this chapter).

If you are an OEM hoping to offer a mobility-as-a-service proposition by leveraging autonomous vehicle technology, your traditional competitors (like other OEMs) will probably be starting from the same position as you are. They will likely have competency in manufacturing and may have a dealer network for distributing cars—but it is also probably the case that they will lack the deep capabilities required for the mobility-as-a-service proposition. Similarly, if you are a component player, your traditional competitors will likely be other component players—who will be in the same boat as OEMs. On the other hand, if you are a software or hardware platform player, your traditional competitors may be starting from a more advantageous position since they have the software platform capabilities needed to drive next-generation propositions like mobility as a service. (But on the other hand, if that's the case, you will likely have those capabilities, too.)

So, with the exception of software platform players, the traditional competitors of the various players we have been discussing in this example are likely not to have many strengths that they can leverage in the context of a mobility-as-a-service proposition. In many cases, these players tend to have a hard time adapting to emerging customer needs and an expanding customer base. They would do well, therefore, to think seriously about ecosystem-based partnerships. Some of these traditional competitors may have ambitious plans and may attempt bold new moves—whether or not they would be successful is an entirely different matter, but nevertheless, it is good practice to keep track of them.

Step 3b: New competitors

In step 3b, we shift our focus from traditional competitors to emerging, ecosystem-based competitors. Who might these competitors be? What are their strengths and weaknesses? How might they evolve to meet emerging customer needs and an evolving customer base? When we speak of emerging ecosystem competitors, we mean competitors who haven't yet been in the space much—if at all—but are beginning to leverage some of the emerging tech and consumer trends we discussed above.

In our automotive example, this sort of emerging competitor might be a cloud player with a software platform-based play that is also looking to offer mobility as a service. It could also be rideshare platform players making similar software platform-based plays. These sorts of players have several advantages in meeting customer needs. For starters, they likely have a data advantage—chances are they have been collecting substantial quantities of data about customers and other factors that could give them valuable insights into the mobility space. They will also have a huge first-mover advantage. One of the advantages of creating or helping to create an ecosystem is that, if done right, there will likely be little need for another ecosystem in the same area. We have repeatedly seen that whenever a set of players tries to develop new ecosystems centered in a particular area, only a handful tend to gain any real traction. And in most areas, there tend to be no more than two to three ecosystems that ultimately emerge, as it becomes harder and harder for new players to build their own ecosystem and move in. This has been true, for instance, in businesses like rideshare, package delivery, and food delivery. However, even once a handful of players have established themselves, it is not uncommon that newer entrants would be able to establish their own sub-ecosystems within the existing, more dominant ecosystems.

Several of the automotive players we have been considering—an OEM, component player, and a sub-systems player—are all likely to face fierce competition from emerging ecosystem players leveraging technologies like EVs and establishing new infrastructure like charging networks and mobile repair networks. Other emerging competitors may use software platforms to establish new ecosystems around autonomous vehicles and other services (e.g., financial players underwriting assets, OEMs providing cars and/or car manufacturing services, hardware players like camera and Lidar manufactures and silicon platform players providing critical components).

Step 3c: Competitive stance

The last part of this step, 3c, involves determining your competitive posture. What is your position relative to these competitors—both traditional and emerging, but especially the emerging ecosystem competitors? What ground can you stake out that will enable you to create better propositions than your ecosystem competitors—especially in the context of shifting customer needs and an evolving customer base? In our automotive example, if you are an OEM or component player, there are a few places where your historical competencies will give you a considerable advantage—for example, in manufacturing, repair and maintenance, and others. You could assume a competitive posture building on these strengths. On the other hand, you could also try to stake out a competitive posture by betting on new capabilities like developing a software platform or an auto software operating system—and building your ecosystem around those. Doing so, however, would be an uphill battle. There are few success stories of this sort of player developing a new or alternate ecosystem, especially when someone else has a first-mover advantage.

And again, it is important to anticipate how your ecosystem competitors' business models may shift and change the nature of the competition. Take, for instance, a software platform player or cloud player offering a mobility-as-a-service proposition. This player may be able to modify its proposition by incorporating advertising into the living-room-on-wheels concept—perhaps offering rides at a reduced price if users agree to having ads interspersed in their digital entertainment content. Or perhaps other players will find a way to collect valuable data that could be monetized in some other business areas—thus offsetting the price of the ride for the customer. OEMs and other more traditional automotive industry players would be far less able to adapt to such a business model.

Overall, step 3 is about anticipating and getting out ahead of other players—especially ecosystem players. We've already invoked Wayne Gretzky's idea of going to where the puck will be instead of where it is—but this is not enough. You also need to be able to predict where the other players will be, and whether they are anticipating the puck's movements as accurately as you are. Doing so means going beyond the sort of planning that companies are already doing—and many companies, to their credit, are already focusing not just on their direct competitors and industry rivals, but on potential new ecosystems competitors, too. The problem is that in many cases, these companies are doing so only superficially. Perhaps competition from Amazon or Google will come up from time to time in board meetings, but the very real threat of cross-sectoral competition from a whole host of different players is not taken seriously enough. Furthermore, instead of the traditional metrics that you use to analyze your direct sectoral competitors, you need to start thinking in terms of non-traditional metrics. Rather than market share, look at relationship market share. What innovative and alternative economic models might your competitors be using? Creator-focused models? Equity sharing models? Or traditional ad-based revenue models? To truly see around the corner and anticipate ecosystem competition, you need to ask questions like these of potential competitors both inside and outside of your sector.

Step 4: Repeat the Cycle

Now that we have taken you through the first three steps of our process for evolving your proposition and choosing where to play, hopefully you are beginning to see that doing so is not only a matter of avoiding negative outcomes—but that it can also be an exciting, imaginative process of building something new and finding innovative ways of creating value. It is equally important that this creative aspect of the process continue on past the early stages. As we said at the outset, step 4 is to repeatedly revisit the first three steps of the process and to reassess the insights you gained from them. Begin by doing this a few times at the outset—repeat the exercises and thought processes several times to be sure you are choosing the right path forward. But even then, you should revisit this process once or twice a year to make sure you are still on the right path as the landscape shifts around you.

The thing you must understand about building and developing an ecosystem mindset is that the work is never done. Indeed, it cannot be successful unless it is an adaptive and dynamic process. It is not simply a matter of creating a plan and executing it. Having a basic sense of what you'd like to accomplish at the outset is critical, of course—but you can't be wedded to that vision. You must always be ready to jump in and adjust as variables shift and the picture gets more complicated— which it invariably will. If we look at some of the most successful ecosystem players today, none of them had a perfect vision of where they were going—but each trusted their instincts and understood that for every step back, there would be two steps forward. Looking back in hindsight on some of these success stories, it's easy to be biased and conclude that the companies' every move was part of a brilliant master plan, but in reality it was a much more experimental, improvisational process. As you continue to think about evolving your proposition, you will want to begin with some generalized plans for how to proceed, but you should also be prepared to depart from them when needed.

Above all, you need to keep up the effort—you will inevitably encounter inertia within your organization, and it is vital that you resist it. This is why you need to continually revisit the customer assessment, the ecosystem assessment, and the competitive assessment—perhaps as frequently as once every few quarters. You need, for example, to keep hiring new people to keep your perspective fresh—and especially people from a wide variety of different backgrounds and sectors. Even if you're not hiring them, meet with people from other companies and other sectors—keep your finger on the pulse of what is happening in other areas. Always have dedicated resources entirely focused on scouring the market to look for potential unexpected competitors—players who may, unbeknownst to you, or perhaps even themselves, be amassing valuable data or some other advantage.

To get a more acute sense of your own vulnerabilities and competitive blind spots, you might want to consider a more narrowly focused approach to anticipating your potential competitors' moves. Specifically, you might consider a war-gaming exercise—a simulated competition, during which you establish certain baseline conditions, plan your moves, and anticipate your competitors' countermoves. The goal is to think multiple steps ahead—to consider not just what you would do given a dozen different moves on the part of your competitor, but what they would do in response, and how you would counter the response, and so on. When this exercise is undertaken seriously, it can look more like a board game: you divide your management group into opposing teams, develop different strategies, decide how each would react to the other's moves, and simulate outcomes. This sort of exercise is, of course, commonly used by militaries, which is why it is called war-gaming.

At the same time, you might also consider a more defensively oriented exercise. By no means does this necessitate taking a more passive, less vigilant approach. On the contrary, it means actively anticipating how your competitors would go about destroying your business—and taking preemptive action to protect yourself. This, of course, is the classic concept of a red team strategy session (sometimes also called "black hat" strategy)—the idea is to put together a group of your best people to think like the competition and brainstorm all of the ways your adversaries might seek to exploit your vulnerabilities. The results of such an exercise can be incredibly alarming—and thus extremely valuable and informative.

At its core, step 4 is about making sure that the insights of the three previous steps are not misunderstood or misdirected. Developing an ecosystem mindset is not simply a matter of spending a few days or even a few weeks thinking about your business from a cross-sectoral perspective—rather, it requires constantly reevaluating your preconceptions, stretching outside your comfort zone, and asking yourself tough questions. It requires coming back and going through the same steps again and again on a regular basis.

EXAMPLE 2: COMFORT AND SECURITY AS A SERVICE

Hopefully, by now, the power of this process is becoming clear. Now that we've explained it in more detail, let's step back and look at the process through the lens of a somewhat different example. Imagine, this time, that you are a narrowly focused player in the home space. You may be, for example, a supplier of heating, ventilation, and air conditioning (HVAC) equipment. Or perhaps you are a supplier of devices like thermostats or security cameras. Or a cloud player trying to make a software/hardware platform-based play in the home market. Or a gas or electricity utility company. Or even a contractor or distributor or installer that enables the go-to-market arm of this sub-sector.

Step 1

The first step, we will recall, is about assessing your current value propositions, your customers' needs, and your customer base. Given the tech and other trends we have covered earlier, how is your customer base shifting? How are their needs shifting? And what does that tell you about how you should evolve your propositions? To answer these questions from the perspective of a player in the home space, we need to think about how tech and consumer trends are shaping and will continue to shape this space in the future. As the cost of computing and data storage goes down, it becomes easier and cheaper for companies to monitor homes, collect data, and analyze them in order to maximize the efficiency of different systems in the home, like heating, electricity, internet, and smart home functionality. It also becomes easier and cheaper for players to store large quantities of data needed for security systems (e.g., surveillance video).

At the same time, customer needs in the home safety and comfort space are evolving in interesting ways. For starters, customers are becoming significantly more concerned with sustainability—they are much more interested in being able to track their energy usage and find ways to improve efficiency with new, high-tech tools. They are also becoming quite accustomed to as-a-service propositions—and expectant of the convenience these propositions bring. Again, when a person can summon a ride in moments via their phone or place an order for dish soap with a voice command for same-day delivery, that person is eventually going to come to expect the same level of convenience in every area of their life.

As home safety and comfort services evolve, the customer base will end up shifting as well. Consider a heating, ventilation, and air conditioning (HVAC) player, for instance. Traditionally, this sort of player has sold equipment through several intermediaries: first, to a distributor, who would then sell to a contractor, who would sell to homeowners. So if you are an equipment player looking to establish an as-a-service type offer, you could very well end up expanding your customer base to include direct consumers—that is to say, your customer base would no longer consist entirely of distributors and contractors, but also homeowners or perhaps other players offering this service.

Next, we consider how to evolve your propositions based on the changing customer needs and customer base. In this evolving landscape of tech and consumer trends, both in the short and long term, there are a number of attractive propositions that can meet current and future customer needs. One that stands out in particular is the proposition of comfort and safety as a service—meaning that customers pay a fee at regular intervals, and in return, you guarantee that parameters such as temperature and humidity will be kept within a certain range at all times within a defined space (like the home) and that the premises will be monitored and kept secure. We could imagine, for example, that a gas or electricity utility company might be drawn to a proposition like this, and choose to expand by offering customers a simple solution that combines the same gas or electricity service they've sold all along with other highly valuable home services such as security.

There are many different ways this proposition could manifest. For example, it might encompass a sub-ecosystem centered on the proposition of maintenance-as-a-service, which would include creating digital twins of customers' homes to help monitor, diagnose, and maintain all systems and equipment within the home. This proposition would involve leveraging the latest technology developments in augmented reality and virtual reality with AI and machine-learning capabilities to create exact digital models of equipment within the home for monitoring and maintaining. Pulling this off would require capabilities from multiple sectors of the economy. For example, for the comfort-as-a-service part of the proposition, you would need capabilities from the HVAC sector, cloud capabilities from the tech sector, and new business models and financing capabilities from the financial sector. In other words, you would need to create a cross-sector ecosystem.

Once you have generated some different potential propositions, it's time to prioritize them. To do this, ask yourself where you might have differentiated capabilities or some special advantage that would give you a leg up in any of these propositions. This sort of advantage could include, for example, access to privileged data, a first-mover advantage, having proprietary technology, or established relationships with customers. By analyzing these advantages, you can determine where you have the potential to provide the most value. This may involve leveraging your own capabilities, leveraging other players within your sector, or leveraging players across other sectors. If, for example, you are a cloud player, and you are sitting on a set of data related to consumers' behaviors and preferences in the home—this would be a significant advantage in building a comfort and security-as-a-service proposition.

Step 2

As we move on to the second step of our process, we need to determine whether any existing ecosystems could be capable of fulfilling the comfort-and-security-as-a-service proposition. Suppose you are an equipment manufacturer hoping to make this proposition. You may have numerous existing vendor/supplier-customer relationships (e.g., contractors, distributors) and supply chain partners (e.g., component players, software players)—but these capabilities and partners are almost certain to fall short of constituting a true ecosystem that can collectively realize the comfort-and-safety-as-a-service proposition. They could, however, eventually be part of an ecosystem if you are able to create one. To successfully do that, you would need a wider variety of partners, including software platform players, financial players, and others. Or suppose you are a gas or electricity utility company hoping to expand from simply providing gas or electricity to offering a comfort-and-security-as-a-service proposition. In this case, you would already have one of the core components needed to heat customers' homes, but you would lack many other necessary capabilities, like cloud systems, software platforms, air-conditioning equipment and many others. To successfully carry out such an expansion, you would need to assemble an ecosystem that pulls all of these elements together.

If you find that there simply are no existing ecosystems that can meet the shifting customer needs—ask yourself: What ecosystems are needed? What ecosystem gap do you need to fill? Consider a software platform player or a cloud player—if such a player wanted to offer a comfort-and-security-as-a-service proposition, it may need to assemble an ecosystem of partners that include a heating and air-conditioning equipment manufacturer, potentially a financial player with financing or asset/risk underwriting expertise, and others.

Step 3

In the third step, we try to anticipate what sort of ecosystem competition we will see in the future, given the tech and consumer changes we've observed. Start by taking a look at your traditional competitors—the players you have competed with historically. How might they evolve as times change? If you are an equipment manufacturer trying to get into the comfort-and-security-as-a-service proposition, this would mean studying other equipment manufacturers. Like you, these players likely have competency in manufacturing and may have a contractor and distributor network for getting equipment where it needs to go and installing it. But they are also likely to lack the deep capabilities needed for the comfort-and-security proposition.

Next, we turn our attention to emerging ecosystem-based competitors. That is to say, competitors that haven't yet been in the home space, but are beginning to leverage some of the emerging tech and consumer trends. For example, cloud-based software or platform players may emerge as potential competitors in the comfort-and-safety-as-a-service proposition. Some of these players may be getting involved by buying companies that are already established in the home space, like hardware or component players, while others may be doing so by partnering with existing service providers, like home security companies. In fact, some cloud-based players, building on a data advantage, are probably already starting to leverage ecosystems, either by putting together their own ecosystems or piggy-backing on ecosystems developed for other purposes. As they continue to do so, they are likely to have some important advantages. For example, they are likely to already have experience with as-a-service propositions in other areas. They may even have the potential to change the basis of competition in the home space by developing new and different ways of getting compensated—by creating entirely new and potentially radically different business models. For example, a cloud player offering comfort and security as a service may choose to bundle that service with other cloud services—or even subsidize one service with the proceeds from the other. They may also choose to bring other revenue sources like data collection or advertising into the mix in an effort to offer customers a better price point. All of this would put more traditional players at an extreme disadvantage.

Finally, after judging the strengths and weaknesses of your traditional and emerging competitors, you need to figure out your own position. Where can you make a differentiated play with the ecosystem to meet the emerging needs of customers and an evolving customer base? If you are an equipment or component player hoping to offer comfort and safety as a service, you will likely have a few areas of historical competency that will prove advantageous like manufacturing, repair and maintenance, and others. You could also try to stake out a competitive posture by betting on a few emerging skills like software platform development and build your ecosystem around those skills.

Finally, at the end of this process, it is a good idea to go through the steps a few more times to be completely sure you are on the right path. If you find yourself coming back to the same propositions again and again, that is a good sign that you are ready to proceed. But even after you have arrived at a workable proposition and begun to assemble the ecosystem you need to enact it, you will want to continually revisit this process on a regular basis. For example, if you create a comfort-and-safety-as-a-service proposition today, it may be the case that in a few years, climate change will significantly alter what your customers' comfort needs are. If heatwaves and other extreme weather events become much more common (as we discussed in Chapter 3), that may change the way you think about your service and how you calibrate your ecosystem.

EXAMPLE 3: INTEGRATED SMALL BUSINESS SERVICES

By now, you've probably internalized the process, but just to make its power absolutely clear, let's explore one more example. Imagine, this time, that you are a business that serves small and medium enterprises (SMEs). Again, as we've done in the previous examples, let's think of this as a somewhat generic business—but it could be, for instance, a financial institution, a telecom, an IT provider, or an insurance company.

Again, following the same process we have in the previous examples, in step 1, we ask: How are your customers' needs changing, and what does that mean for you? As a provider to SMEs, the number one need you are serving is the need for convenience—the need to have all the basics taken care of together, all at once, so they don't have to occupy a great deal of one's attention. Whether you offer phone and internet service, financial services, or insurance to small businesses, these businesses—your clients—are increasingly seeing your offering as a low priority, a necessary evil. They want to focus on getting new customers, new revenues, and whatever creative offering is the core of their business. What they *don't* want to focus on is you. These preferences are getting more and more acute as these small businesses face stiffer and stiffer competition—leaving less time for dealing with service providers—and as digitization accelerates, making it easier and easier for services like yours to be automated and combined with other services. At the same time, market disrupters are increasingly coming in with integrated value propositions—and can easily take over your clients, given that the type of service you offer doesn't foster an especially close customer relationship. Increasingly, what you are really competing for is not small business banking or small business telecom services, but rather customer ownership of these small businesses.

The upshot is this: regardless of how much energy you put into your offering, your services are increasingly getting commoditized and are back of mind for your clients. If this trend continues, it should be clear to you that it will lead to continued margin compression, and you will ultimately be disintermediated by emerging platforms that can truly capture the interests of these SMEs. Ultimately, you are facing disintermediation, disaggregation, commoditization, and being made invisible.

This is, to put it mildly, a very difficult situation. So how can you evolve your proposition to better meet your clients' changing needs? The only way to get out of the trap is to build a closer relationship with your small business clients—and one of the best ways to do that is to expand, to create a platform that integrates a whole host of services like your own, services that small businesses need but don't want to focus too much attention on. In doing this, you stand to become an indispensable tool for small business owners or managers—a portal through which they can access all manner of services that SMEs might need: banking, telecom services, insurance, legal services, administration, HR, accounting, business intelligence, tech support, and more. Building such a platform would even open up the possibility of creating entirely new services—for instance, you could create a social network for SMEs (beyond what's offered today by traditional social networking players), allowing them to speak to one another, share information, and compare tactics. We could call this whole proposition integrated small business services, incorporating services you provide yourself alongside third-party services offered by partners or subsidiaries that you serve to your clients through your platform. Of course, such a proposition would need to compete against services from current cloud and online players, but the idea would be to get ahead by offering simplicity and convenience beyond what others have been able to do.

This has the potential to be quite lucrative. First of all, these small businesses are often so pressed for time that they will very likely be open to paying a high premium for convenience. But also, you can build productive and rewarding relationships with the third parties on your platform as well, since they have a huge customer acquisition cost and will be willing to pay big commissions for new customers, which you would be able to offer them thanks to the strength of your integrated platform.

It's important, however, to remember that businesses are slow to change their behavior. Creating an integrated small business services proposition will be enormously helpful in attracting SME customers, but doing so will not be enough by itself. To win customers and drive growth, you will need a central, extremely powerful and distinct service to serve as your lynchpin, around which you will situate all your other services. You could, for example, build a marketplace of sorts catering to the highly specialized needs of small business, in order to

Next, in step 3, you need to assess the potential ecosystem
petition for your small business services proposition. Your
itional competitors—other banks, telecoms, insurance compa-
, and so forth—may also be thinking about expanding to meet
r customers' changing needs, but may lack key capabilities
ded to build a platform and attract third-party providers to be
of their ecosystem. In all likelihood, new market disrupters
ing in with integrated value propositions will be a much
ater threat. These players, which may include tech companies,
id providers, or software platform providers, will likely
ady have significant digital capabilities and thus a head start
building an integrated services platform. They may also have
blished relationships with third-party providers that they
ld bring into their ecosystem. As the borders between the tra-
onal sectors of the economy continue to fade away, we are
ly to see more and more of these integrated attackers making
s-sectoral plays.

And finally, in step 4, you will need to go back and repeat steps 1
ough 3 in a structured way. Again, this is both to ensure you have
ved at the best possible set of answers for the short term, but also
keep your approach flexible and attuned to changing circum-
ces. For example, as more and more businesses become involved
cosystems, this will likely change the needs of small businesses
thus will alter how you, as a B2B services player, think about your
position.

As we pointed out earlier, the three examples we have discussed
his chapter have all involved hypothetical, generic companies. We
this to illustrate the many different angles from which different
ds of players may approach the task of adapting to the ecosystem
nomy. But telling the story this way risks giving the impression
t these processes are all abstract or theoretical—that no one has
ally used them successfully in the real world. This could not be
her from the truth.

In fact, in the real world, there are already *many* examples of com-
ies that have successfully built full ecosystem models—or are on
ir way. Many of these players have used a version of the process
described above to start on their journey and have achieved mean-
ful success—and we are not speaking only of tech companies and
tups, but of incumbents, too. Consider, for example, OTP, a Central
ropean bank, which realized in the early 2010s that it would be

ultimately help those businesses find new cus
Alternatively, your anchor could be an integratec
SMEs that brings together revenues, payments, cas
and more. Finally, you could also center your proj
form for up-and-coming businesses, helping them
challenges and specific needs of building a busines
up: first and foremost, help finding funding, but also
ing talent and co-founders, business registry, wek
ments, accounting, and banking. By combining thes
into a single integrated proposition, you could giv
nesses everything they need to scale up and meet th

Once you have assembled a range of different op
your proposition, the next step is to prioritize and na
based on where you may possess differentiated cap
other special advantage. For example, if you are a ba
tionally given business loans to SMEs, you may hav
experience working with new businesses and have
quantity of data about their needs and tendencies. Th
uable advantage in pursuing a startup-centered sm
vices platform. If you are an IT provider—or, especi
cloud service provider—you may already have a l
capabilities needed to deploy an integrated services
you a huge leg up in pursuing any of these propositic

In step 2 of our process, you need to assess ec
What is the ecosystem gap that you need to fill? Pa
making a design choice: vertical or horizontal? Do yc
small businesses in a single sector and focus on their
Or do you want to offer a single, specialized categor
businesses from many different sectors? A vertical
services proposition would be best suited to clients w
idiosyncratic. Consider the needs of a farmer, for exar
quite specific: weather data, agronomic advice, info
mate change and regenerative farming, and much n
the needs of a doctor or medical practice are also very
administration needs, a connection to private and sta
ance systems, diagnostics, and pharmacogenomics. A
horizontal small business services proposition would
ing one specific category of services to a wide varie
kinds of businesses.

unable to keep its younger customers with only pure banking offers. As they soon came to realize, they needed a broader, cross-sectoral proposition—in other words, a commerce ecosystem play.

OTP began by searching for compelling customer propositions to target the segment of customers they wanted to attract. In so doing, they quickly realized that in order to make those propositions compelling, they would need an ecosystem. The proposition they ultimately devised included ticket booking services for movies, festivals, public transportation, and many other functions—all under a platform called Simple. By creating a broad, integrated ecosystem, the bank was able to capture the market and retain and grow their customer base, particularly within their target demographic of younger people.

Discovery, a South African insurer, provides another example. Discovery used a similar process to reinvent its health value proposition, finding unserved customer needs and addressing them from an ecosystem perspective. Vitality, which is the company's science-based behavior change program, orchestrates an ecosystem of healthy eating, fitness and health services, with active customer relations and a loyalty points program at its heart. On top of the substantial economic value creation that Discovery has achieved, it has also contributed to positive health outcomes for customers, adding (by Discovery's calculations) up to ten or even twelve years to customers' life expectancy. Many other companies are still in the earlier stages of building ecosystem businesses: they have identified the ecosystem where they want to play and the value proposition they want to create—but have not yet fully proven it, and thus remain somewhere in the implementation phase, as described later in this book.

While each of the examples we've explored in this chapter involve very different services and needs—in mobility, in the home, and in B2B services—each also offers a powerful picture of the new value you can create if you embrace the ecosystem mindset.

But to get to a place where you can create that value, you need to set yourself up for success—you need to determine where you should play and how you should evolve your proposition. Now that we have shown you how to do that, it's time to move on and start asking some deeper questions—specifically about yourself, and what role you are meant to play in the new ecosystem you are imagining. This will be the topic of Chapter 5.

THINGS TO WATCH OUT FOR WHEN CHOOSING WHERE TO PLAY

When you are determining where to play and how to evolve your proposition to be competitive in the emerging ecosystem economy, you should avoid making the few following mistakes.

1. Failing to achieve a quantum leap of experience for all key stakeholders

Many companies contemplating where to play in the ecosystem economy have incredible, innovative ideas for expanding their proposition. But what they oftentimes fail to realize is that unless their ideas can achieve a quantum leap of customer experience improvement, they won't be successful. You need to not only make life easier for your customer—you need to make life *vastly* easier. The same is true of other stakeholders in your ecosystem. Adding a few superficial partnerships, or an additional service here, or a new form of connectivity there—this most certainly will not be enough to make a meaningful difference in customers' lives. Ecosystems are not a collection of loosely affiliated services on a web page—they need to be deeply integrated, fully end-to-end value propositions. Think from a customer's perspective about how much better a service needs to be than the competition to truly stand out. You cannot tinker around the edges—you need to achieve transformative change. Lastly, when you think about improvements, make sure you consider every key stakeholder, not just your customers. For example, in the ecosystem context, make sure you focus on significantly improving the experience for your partners, too.

2. Losing sight of customer segmentation and focus

The second area where companies frequently err when deciding where to play is in customer segmentation. One of the best ways to build an ecosystem, especially if you are an incumbent and lack the sort of technological edge that new startups often have, is to focus intently on a specific segment of customers. Not to do all things for all customers, but to meaningfully improve specific kinds of experiences for specific kinds of customers. This means going deep to understand customer needs, building a proposition around the end-to-end customer journey, and solving customer pain points. It is much better to achieve a significant improvement of experience for a portion of your customers than a marginal improvement of experience for a large portion of your customers.

3. Losing focus on building a positive upward spiral of ongoing engagement

Most companies today are not sufficiently attentive to building a positive, self-reinforcing, upward spiral of ongoing customer engagement. This is the magic behind many successful ecosystem businesses, whether we're talking about Amazon, or Tencent, or Apple—each creates a cycle in which engagement, data, and emotional connection help to get customers more deeply involved in the ecosystem and more engaged with its products and services. More engagement means more customers using your products and services—and ultimately, more interactions. This increase in interactions, in turn, generates more data for you to collect, which you can use to tailor your offerings more precisely to your customers' needs and desires. And the better you are able to shape your offerings to their idiosyncrasies, the deeper the connection you will be able to develop with them. This fuels the whole cycle anew—a deeper connection means more engagement and more interactions. The spiral continues on and on—upward ever higher.

However, many companies are missing out on the huge potential of this positive upward spiral because they are not focused enough on building positive loops of engagement to encourage it. Building a positive loop could mean, for example, creating a so-called network effect by bringing together large groups of participants with elements like a marketplace, social connections, and sticky services like loyalty programs. And there are many other ways to achieve such a network effect.

4. Pursuing profits at the expense of customer value

Finally, the fourth mistake that companies frequently make is that they allow profits to guide their decision about where to play, instead of letting value creation guide that decision. They confuse what the ultimate goal of ecosystems is. Amazon, with its well-documented focus on customer value, is a good example of how to avoid this pitfall.[10] The questions you really need to be asking are: How am I truly adding to and improving the value equation for my customers? What positive impact am I delivering? How am I continually improving upon that? In the end, putting your energy and focus into improving value for your customers will yield much better results. Again, when we say *customers*, we use the term in a broader sense that includes users of your service, your partners, and any other relevant stakeholders.

5

It Takes a Village

Finding Your Place in the Ecosystem, Choosing Your Role, and Picking the Right Collaborators

As we continue our journey through the world of ecosystems, we now turn our attention from the question of *where* to play to the question of *with whom?* In the previous chapter, we gave you a framework for evolving your proposition and choosing where to play in the rapidly changing ecosystem economy. This process, you will recall, began with looking at technology and consumer trends, assessing how they will affect your proposition, and finding a way to move forward by leveraging that change. It then continued with an assessment of existing and emerging ecosystems, a sizing up of the competition, and an iterative process of continual reevaluation to account for shifting circumstances.

Now it is time to take this process one level deeper. The key questions you need to answer now are: What role should you play in the ecosystem? And which other businesses will you need to collaborate with? An ecosystem, after all, is by definition a *community* of interconnected businesses that work across the boundaries between traditional sectors . An important part of what makes ecosystems special, therefore, is that they thrive on connectivity. They create value through cooperation and then share that value among their different constituent parts.

So—if you can't do it on your own, where does that leave you? Who will your collaborators be? What position will you take among them? What sort of relationships will you have with them?

ORCHESTRATORS AND PARTICIPANTS

We begin with the question of roles. When businesses take part in an ecosystem, they must cooperate with others. This cooperation, however, is almost invariably guided by some sort of structure, and businesses can play a number of different roles within that structure. Generally speaking, though, these roles fall into two main categories: orchestrators and participants. It is worth taking a moment to explore each of these archetypal roles in more detail.

To be an orchestrator is to be the crux of the ecosystem—the central player that brings together the other participants. As the orchestrator, you typically have the responsibility to lead, organize, and evolve the ecosystem in order to make it as effective and efficient as possible. At the same time, you also bear the responsibility of maintaining the ecosystem's platform or backbone, drawing in new participants and customers, and ensuring that the ecosystem as a whole remains an attractive, dynamic space where other players will want to continue doing business. Being a participant, on the other hand, means joining an ecosystem formulated by someone else and agreeing to their terms. Being a participant can bring enormous benefits, like the convenience of an already-established customer interface and access to a potentially much wider customer base—but it also comes at some cost, including in many cases sharing a percentage of the value you collectively create with the ecosystem orchestrator.

Here are some of the key features that set orchestrators apart:

- **Platform:** First, they have some sort of digital or physical platform or common thread that others can leverage to build, distribute, or enhance their own products and services. This platform frequently takes the form of a backbone, operating system, or marketplace.

- **Community Organizing:** Orchestrators function as community organizers of sorts—which is to say, they recruit, attract, coordinate, and retain the community of participants. They enforce community standards and seek feedback to better themselves and their platforms.

- **Customer Network and Go-to-Market Infrastructure:** Orchestrators use their platforms to create a network effect, connecting participants with customers and sometimes with one another. In other words, they help ecosystem participants thrive by bringing them together and providing services to help them enhance their offers as well as access to a broad network of customers. As more and more customers join, the ecosystem becomes more and more attractive to participants. And likewise, as more and more participants join, the ecosystem becomes increasingly attractive to customers.

- **Resources:** Orchestrators typically provide a set of resources to help participants build propositions and ultimately fit into their ecosystem. These resources could include, for example, a software developer kit, a product development kit, cybersecurity services, billing and collection infrastructure, or a customer feedback mechanism, to name just a few.

- **Improvement Trajectory:** For the good of all parties involved in the ecosystem, orchestrators tend to continually look for ways to enhance the platform's proposition, to innovate, and to deploy new business models.

- **Robust Framework for Relationships:** Typically, orchestrators use a variety of different business models to structure their relationships with their participants. These could include, for example, models in which orchestrators share the upside with participants, models in which participants pay a flat fee to join the ecosystem, equity sharing models in which orchestrators share value in the form of equity, or models in which the platform is open source and free to everyone. For any of these arrangements, orchestrators also typically set up a framework to manage the relationship.

Similarly, we can identify some of the most important attributes that distinguish the role of being a participant. As you might expect, these attributes are the converse of the qualities that define orchestrators:

- **User of the Platform:** By definition, participants rely on someone else's backbone or platform. Just as possessing this platform typically defines the role of orchestrator, lacking one typically defines the role of participant. The participant's degree of reliance can vary, but in nearly every case, it is true that they would be unable to fulfill key parts of their value proposition without access to such a platform or backbone—either digital or physical, or sometimes a combination of the two.

- **Building on Top of a Platform:** Typically, participants build their value proposition on top of the orchestrator's platform or leverage the orchestrator's platforms and tools to offer their own products and services. In some cases, they help to enhance the platform by contributing to its evolution.

- **Go-to-Market Infrastructure:** Participants also frequently leverage the infrastructure of the platform provider or use it to augment their own go-to-market infrastructure. This could include access to sales and marketing channels, customer feedback channels, and customer service channels.

- **Adherence to Relationship Framework:** Participants join ecosystems by entering into agreements with orchestrators. Participants thus have fewer commitments and responsibilities, but the agreements can limit their flexibility and require them to follow rules set by the orchestrator. The agreements also generally involve sharing the value they will collectively create with the orchestrator. For example, the agreement may stipulate that the orchestrator will take a portion of any sales that the participant generates while leveraging the orchestrator's platform. This percentage would serve as compensation for the use of the platform and access to the tools necessary to craft the value propositions as well additional services like security, billing, collections, and ongoing improvement to the platform.

To take a classic example of these two archetypal roles, consider the iOS and Android app stores. In these cases, Apple and Google are clearly the orchestrators. They each created an environment in which third-party app developers can sell their software and various propositions to consumers. The third-party developers are, of course, the participants, and in return for the privilege of using Apple and Google's platforms to sell their apps, they pay a percentage of every sale.[1] However, Apple and Google must work for that percentage—they provide app developers with resources like software developer kits; they continually work to make their platforms stronger, more reliable, and more secure; and, most importantly, they connect the third-party developers to a vast pool of customers who use their platforms. Each party provides something the other needs—Apple and Google could not sustain healthy app marketplaces without the help of third-party developers to build an abundance of apps, and the third-party developers in many cases could not survive without a robust network to help get their apps to customers—and all the surrounding infrastructure.

Another case that does a good job of illustrating this dynamic is that of ridesharing companies like Uber and Lyft. Much like futuristic, autonomous vehicle-driven mobility-as-a-service propositions that we discussed in the previous chapter, these companies have created platforms that enable third-party car owners and drivers to connect to customers. Uber and Lyft function as orchestrators, building their respective communities, providing resources to help drivers, and—critically—connecting them with customers. The drivers, in turn, are the participants, and provide the core service of mobility to the customers. Each party—the platform operators and the third-party participants—provides something critical for the other. But the platforms serve the central function of coordinating activities, structuring the relationship, and providing the backbone. For example, they provide billing and collection as well as ensuring the safety and security of all parties involved.[2]

The prospect of being an orchestrator is attractive in many ways, but it also comes with some real responsibility—and more than a few headaches. The advantages are clear: not only do you get to control your own destiny and influence your network of participants, but by virtue of having created the ecosystem, you are entitled to ask those participants to compensate you for the enormous benefits you are providing. They are reliant on you—and it is in their interest to keep working hard to hold up their end of the bargain. And yet, at the same time, there are reasons why some may find orchestrating unappealing. Starting an ecosystem from scratch can be an enormous undertaking, requiring a considerable investment of time, energy, and resources. For those unwilling or unable to make the necessary tradeoffs and commitments, such an endeavor may prove disastrous. Half measures are almost certain to result in disappointment—to be truly successful, you must go all in. And the task is not over by any means once your ecosystem is established. Although you will enjoy a first-mover advantage, you will also have to continue expending effort and committing resources to maintain the ecosystem, update the platform, and keep everything running smoothly.

On the other hand, being a participant may seem like a constrained position: as a participant, you are reliant on an external entity for many needs, you are devoting a portion of your value to paying for the privilege of participating in the ecosystem, and you don't have the freedom to do as you please in every respect. You are obliged to work within the confines of the orchestrator's rules. Mere participation, however, has its advantages. Without having to make the considerable investments required to build a new ecosystem, participants are afforded a relatively straightforward path to developing new solutions and value propositions—and will be able to do so quickly.

This essential relationship between orchestrators and participants can be governed by several different business models, which can have a significant impact on how effectively each player fits into the ecosystem. For example, some ecosystems employ a simple business model in which participants pay a flat fee to be a part of an orchestrator's ecosystem—they are, effectively, paying for a service. More sophisticated ecosystems often use a business model in which the participants and orchestrators share the value they are creating together—sometimes even with their users. Even more sophisticated ecosystems will use a model of equity sharing, in which an orchestrator and several participants collectively develop a value proposition, and then the orchestrator shares the upside with participants in the form of equity. Other ecosystems employ an open-source business model, in which participants don't pay the orchestrator, but instead contribute to the betterment of the platform. These ecosystems are in many cases free and open to almost any interested participant, but in return for the use of the ecosystem's backbone, there is an expectation that they will share any improvements they are able to make with the larger community.

In the end, while each position has its plusses and minuses, what is most important is that you cultivate an ecosystem mindset. Even if you lack the capacity to orchestrate, or if you are unable to build an ecosystem-oriented business, learning to *think* in terms of ecosystems will prove immeasurably helpful. Doing so will expand your horizons and help you to evaluate your own propositions with clear eyes so that you can evolve them to stay ahead of your competitors and customers' ever-increasing expectations. And after all, both orchestrators and participants are essential to creating successful ecosystems—one can't live without the other.

SHADES OF GRAY: A SPECTRUM OF ECOSYSTEM ROLES

While the distinction between orchestrators and participants is crucial for understanding the different roles companies can play in an ecosystem, it does not provide the full picture. In reality, the choice between orchestrator or participant is not a simple binary decision. Rather, these archetypal roles are the two ends on a spectrum of options that includes many subtler gradations. This spectrum ranges from extremely active to extremely passive (see Figure 5.1). This is essentially a question of how important you are in the ecosystem for creating value, how much influence you have, and what share of the value generated you are entitled to.

FIGURE 5.1   **Critical steps and highly iterative process to determine what role to play**

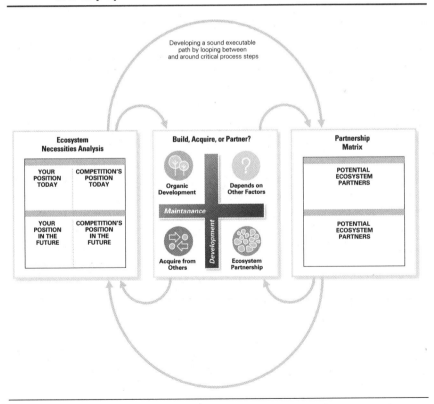

There are a number of in-between roles that companies can occupy between being a pure orchestrator and a plain old participant. For instance, you could be the orchestrator of a sub-ecosystem within someone else's larger ecosystem. Think of the previous examples we gave—Uber and Lyft on the one hand, and Apple and Google's app stores on the other. Ridesharing apps like Uber and Lyft are the orchestrators of their own ecosystems but they are participants within the app-store ecosystems of iOS and Android. In one sense, they coordinate the activities of players within their own ecosystem, but in another, they are subject to someone else's rules.

You could also find yourself in a hybrid role, exercising a great degree of control over one aspect of the ecosystem relationship and less over another—for example, if you are more of a back-office orchestrator, you might have strong control over the data generated by the ecosystem but a much lighter control over the customer relationship. Or conversely, you may have more control over the customer and less over the data. You could be a pure participant, but active in multiple ecosystems. Or, at the far-right end of the spectrum, you could be a plain old participant, active in only one ecosystem, and reliant exclusively on a single orchestrator. As you consider what role is right for you, you can begin by asking yourself some questions. First, take stock of your ambition: Do you *want* to orchestrate an ecosystem? After going through the steps that we described in the previous chapter, you probably have some idea of where you want to play, the competitive posture you would like to assume, and what you need to do to evolve your value proposition. Given that information, what are the challenges specific to orchestrating in your chosen space? Are you ready to face these challenges? It could be that your chosen proposition simply involves too many start-up costs—and you would be better off leveraging a platform that someone else has already built. Above all, you need to ask yourself: Is it *practical* to try to orchestrate a new ecosystem in this space?

Next, assuming you are still interested in orchestrating, consider your own history and strengths—your capabilities, your relationships, your experience and understanding. How strong are your current sector-based relationships? Will they be of any help in building an ecosystem? What capabilities have you developed working in your traditional space? How applicable are these capabilities to the task of orchestrating an ecosystem? What capabilities will you need to successfully pull off the proposition you devised in the previous chapter? Which of these capabilities do you lack? Are there specific strengths you have that are indicative of what sort of an orchestrator you might end up being? For example, do you have especially deep customer relationships? Do you have a valuable data set that reveals some important insight about your market or your customers? Do you have some other distinctive advantage? Answering these questions honestly will help you begin to determine whether orchestrating is your natural role.

As you continue to deepen your thinking about what role to play, it may be helpful to give some structure to your thoughts. In the remainder of the chapter, we will provide a step-by-step process through which you can figure out which capabilities and assets you will need to successfully develop an ecosystem business; decide how to get them; and then decide which ecosystem partnerships you will need and which other players are best equipped to collaborate with you. These steps are part of a flexible, iterative process—meaning that you can cycle back and forth between the different steps, in multiple rounds, until you have worked out a short list of potential partners (see Figure 5.2).

The first step is to perform what we call an ecosystem necessities analysis, which helps you enumerate and prioritize the different assets and capabilities you will need for your ecosystem. The second step is to determine whether you should build, acquire, or partner in order to attain those necessities. And the third step is to determine, for those assets and capabilities you will need partners to attain, *which* potential collaborators are best positioned to help you.

We begin with the ecosystem necessities analysis. Thinking back to the value proposition you crafted in the previous chapter, make a list of the assets and capabilities you will need to execute it—that is to say, the technical know-how, the hardware or software, the customer base, the vendor relationships, the data, the go-to-market infrastructure. Everything necessary to bring the concept of your value proposition to fruition. As you do this, make sure you take into consideration the evolving consumer behavior and technology landscape. The assets and capabilities that are most frequently needed for ecosystem propositions generally fall into a few categories: platform or backbone capabilities, product/offer capabilities, go-to-market capabilities, and customer capabilities.

Platform or backbone capabilities are those competencies needed to build and maintain a robust digital or physical platform to organize your ecosystem. Product capabilities include those

FIGURE 5.2   **Spectrum of roles in ecosystems**

Plain old participant	Participant in one or multiple ecosystems exclusively	Hybrid role	Orchestrator of sub-ecosystem	Orchestrator of broad ecosystem
A participant in an ecosystem orchestrated by someone else	Participant is exclusive to a single or multiple ecosystems	Participant acts as an orchestrator in some cases and a participant in others	Orchestrating part of a broad ecosystem that is orchestrated by another participant	Orchestrating a broad ecosystem

PLAIN OLD PARTICIPANT

Characteristics

- Reliant on orchestrator's platform
- Builds a value propisition on top of the orchestrator's platform or leveraging orchestrator's tools and resources
- Leverages orchestrator's go-to-market infrastructure
- Adheres to relationship framework set by the orchestrator

Implications

- Fewer start-up costs
- Potentially lower reward compared with an orchestrator

ORCHESTRATOR OF A BROAD ECOSYSTEM

Characteristics

- Provides a platform
- Organizes a community of participants
- Connects participants with network of customers and go-to-market infrastructure
- Provides resources to participants
- Continually works to enhance the ecosystem
- Offers robust framework for relationships

Implications

- Large investment of time, effort, and money
- Higher potential rewards

needed to expand, scale, or improve a product offering, including critical data to improve a product, a key missing piece of technology necessary to enhance the product/service, or some other valuable piece of information or know-how. Go-to-market capabilities include channel presence, access, reach, and relationships. Finally, customer capabilities involve pre- and post-sales service capabilities for your offering. This list is by no means comprehensive, but hopefully it can serve as a jumping-off point for you to think about the capabilities you need for your proposition.

Once you begin to narrow down the list and tailor it to your own case, you can enter it into an ecosystem necessities analysis matrix (Figure 5.3), charting which players (including you) have those capabilities today and which ones might obtain them in the future. Hopefully, seeing all this information assembled will help you determine which roles are best for you—and which roles might be a stretch. If a role is a stretch, that doesn't necessarily mean you should not pursue it—only that you will face additional challenges for which you will need to prepare. And in any case, it will be helpful to understand what's involved and what you will be up against. Orchestrators typically begin from a strong position in at least a few of these key capabilities—and then leverage that advantage to establish themselves and build the ecosystem, which helps them draw in new participants to supply the capabilities they may be lacking.

ECOSYSTEM NECESSITIES ANALYSIS

Having all of this information assembled in one place will give you a foundation from which to select the role that best fits your situation tactically and practically—to decide where on the spectrum you should be. Where do you have a natural ownership and where do you not? In places where you don't—how can you augment your assets and capabilities by bringing in other players?

BUILD, ACQUIRE, OR PARTNER?

While bringing in other players can certainly be effective, it is not necessarily the right choice in every situation. Partnering is a great way to get assets and capabilities that you need—but it is certainly not the only way. You could, for example, develop capabilities internally, on your own, or—if you have the resources—you could acquire an outside company that has already developed them. Picking which of these options makes sense in a given situation can be challenging, but you can begin to assess the situation by weighing a few key factors.

FIGURE 5.3   **Ecosystem necessities analysis**

Platform	POSITION TODAY:		POSITION IN THE FUTURE:	
	YOURS	COMPETITION'S	YOURS	COMPETITION'S
Digital or physical				
Marketplace				
Operating system				

Product/offer capabilities	POSITION TODAY:		POSITION IN THE FUTURE:	
	YOURS	COMPETITION'S	YOURS	COMPETITION'S
Critical pieces of techonology know-how				
Data access and ownership				
Logical product/service extensions to broaden and deepen the offers				

Go-to-Market capabilities	POSITION TODAY:		POSITION IN THE FUTURE:	
	YOURS	COMPETITION'S	YOURS	COMPETITION'S
Channel presence and access				
Depth, breadth, and reach of existing relationships				
Emerging relationships				

Customers	POSITION TODAY:		POSITION IN THE FUTURE:	
	YOURS	COMPETITION'S	YOURS	COMPETITION'S
Customer service pre- and post-sales (resolving issues)				
Customer success — to ensure and drive value delivery for customers with your offer				

Miscellaneous/Other	POSITION TODAY:		POSITION IN THE FUTURE:	
	YOURS	COMPETITION'S	YOURS	COMPETITION'S

Begin by looking back at your ecosystem necessities analysis. Each line item in the matrix, you will recall, represents an asset or capability that is needed to evolve your value proposition as planned in the previous chapter. Each of these assets or capabilities could potentially be obtained by one of several methods: by developing it on your own, by acquiring another business that already has it, or by forming an ecosystem partnership. To decide which path to take in each instance, you must judge the assets and capabilities by two criteria: how difficult they would be to develop on your own, and how difficult they would be to maintain thereafter. When we talk about the difficulty of developing assets and capabilities, we mean assessing how long it would take to do so, what level of resources you would need to put into making it happen, and what level of attention such an endeavor would require. By the difficulty of *maintaining* assets and capabilities, we mean the level of resources and attention that would be required to keep the assets in good working order. When thinking about how difficult an asset or capability would be to maintain, consider: Do you have the technical expertise necessary to continually adapt the new asset or capability to keep up with a constantly changing technology environment? And do you have the wherewithal to manage—at scale—the issues that such an asset or capability may introduce?

Using these two criteria (difficulty to develop and difficulty to maintain), you can begin to sort your ecosystem necessities into different categories: easy to develop and easy to maintain, easy to develop but hard to maintain, and so on. To give some structure to this exercise, you might use a two-by-two grid that we call a build, acquire, or partner grid.

BUILD, ACQUIRE, OR PARTNER GRID

As the grid in Figure 5.4 shows, the relative difficulty of developing or maintaining a particular asset or capability can help identify the best way to go about obtaining it. If a capability is straightforward to develop and doesn't require much effort or know-how to maintain, it should be simple to build organically on your own. If the asset or capability in question is harder to develop but easy to maintain, you might instead consider acquiring an outside business that has already developed it—incorporating their business into your own will save you valuable time. And finally, if you need an asset or capability that is

FIGURE 5.4   **Build, acquire, or partner?**

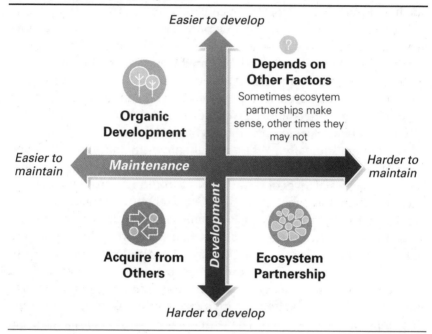

difficult both to develop and to maintain, the best route is likely an ecosystem partnership. Bringing participant businesses with the necessary skills or assets into your ecosystem through a structured collaboration will give you the best of both worlds. You will have access to the capabilities you need without going through the trouble of having to develop or maintain them on your own. This lower-right quadrant of the grid is where we'll focus our attention as we consider potential ecosystem collaborators.

PICKING THE RIGHT COLLABORATORS

After you have figured out the role that best suits you and determined which assets and capabilities are required to assume that role, the next logical step is to determine who else you need in your ecosystem. As we mentioned at the outset of this chapter, ecosystems are necessarily *communities* of different businesses working together. You simply can't do it all on your own. Now it is time to decide what this will look like in practice. Who will your partners be? What will each of you bring to the table? And how will those assets and capabilities work together?

The first thing to understand is that to survive in the new ecosystem economy, you will need to expand both the breadth and depth of your relationships. That is to say, you will need to drastically expand the number of partners you are working with, but you will also need to make those relationships count for more. Many companies today will look at their current partnerships and find ways to convince themselves that they are doing enough. But if they look honestly, they will see they are falling short. In many cases, the ecosystem partnerships they are engaged in are, in fact, surface-level, one-dimensional arrangements—distribution relationships or product relationships, for example. For some, the word *partnerships* has become a means of giving their traditional vendor-customer relationships a sheen of sophistication—a way of pretending that they are building an ecosystem without truly putting in the necessary effort. But if the ecosystem you are building consists entirely of businesses that you are buying things from or selling things to—then it's not really much of an ecosystem, at least the way we define it. One of the fundamental qualities that characterizes this distinction is the presence of collective value creation. That is to say, in real, ecosystem-based relationships, partners grow the pie together and then share that value. The relationship is not transactional, but rather, cooperative.

If we look at all of the different types of partnerships that businesses engage in, we can see a clear distinction between traditional distribution-supplier relationships and the much deeper, strategically integrated, ecosystem-based partnerships (see Figure 5.5).

With all of this in mind, it is important as you assemble your ecosystem that you are clear with yourself about what kind of partnerships you are really engaged in—and what purpose your partners are serving.

The next step is to take the assets and capabilities that require ecosystem partnerships and figure out which potential collaborators are best positioned to help you get them. These are, in other words, the assets and capabilities from the lower-right quadrant of your build, acquire, or partner grid. For each capability or asset that fell into that portion of the grid, create a list of players who currently have it and are well positioned to continue having it in the future. These players can be entered into what we call a partnership matrix (Figure 5.6), along with the different assets and capabilities you hope to leverage to build your ecosystem business.

FIGURE 5.5 **Continuum of partnerships**

Traditional Partnerships	Ecosystem Partnerships

Type of relationship

Supplier, vendor/client	Cooperative partnership

Type of collaboration

Contractual, transational, often arms length	Strategic and deep-rooted, typically build off of each other's capabilities

Value creation

Mostly shifting value rather than growing the whole pie	Growing the overall pie — typically creating new markets

Evolution

More or less static: Terms and relationship stay the same generally	Usually dynamic: Relationships often change or deepen over time

FIGURE 5.6   **Partnership matrix**

Platform	
	POTENTIAL ECOSYSTEM PARTNERS
Digital or physical	
Marketplace	
Operating system	

Product/offer capabilities	
	POTENTIAL ECOSYSTEM PARTNERS
Critical pieces of techonology know-how	
Data access and ownership	
Logical product/service extensions to broaden and deepen the offers	

Go-to-Market capabilities	
	POTENTIAL ECOSYSTEM PARTNERS
Channel presence and access	
Depth, breadth, and reach of existing relationships	
Emerging relationships	

Customers	
	POTENTIAL ECOSYSTEM PARTNERS
Customer service pre- and post-sales (resolving issues)	
Customer success — to ensure and drive value delivery for customers with your offer	

Miscellaneous/Other	
	POTENTIAL ECOSYSTEM PARTNERS

PARTNERSHIP MATRIX

To evaluate the potential collaborators in your partnership matrix, you can use what we call an attractiveness/feasibility analysis. As you might expect, this involves judging each potential partner by two criteria: how attractive they are to you, and the feasibility of the overall collaboration—in other words, "do we want to partner with them?" and "do they want to partner with us?"

Let's begin with attractiveness. There are a few sub-categories that you can examine to evaluate a potential ecosystem partner's attractiveness. First, do they have a large, at-scale, digitally- or non-digitally-active customer base that will allow for rapid, bulk customer acquisition and engagement at a low cost? Or, if they don't, can they help you establish your own at-scale customer base at a low cost? Will their customer base complement your existing customer base in terms of specific targets and segments? Second, consider their data resources. Do they have insightful, end-customer data which complement your existing data set? Do these data provide new insights on consumer behavior and preferences? Can they help you identify potential high-value and underserved customers with a low customer-acquisition cost by leveraging the data? Can they help you develop exciting new products and services with the data they have? Third, think about how adept the potential partner is at reaching their customers. Do they have multiple, meaningful ways of interacting with their customers? And do those touchpoints support customer acquisition, engagement, and back-end operations? Finally, and perhaps most importantly, consider assets and capabilities. Do they have capabilities and assets that will accelerate the development and implementation of partnerships with other players we might need to build our ecosystem? We should stipulate, by the way, that this whole list of criteria and questions to ask is just a starting point in the process of gauging a potential ecosystem partner's attractiveness. There may be many other factors you will want to consider based on your context. But the bottom line is that you need to determine if your potential partner will be able to help you deliver more value for your customers.

Once you've assessed the factors that figure into attractiveness, flip the equation back around and ask yourself if it makes sense for the potential partner to work with you. Again, there are a few sub-factors you can reference to make this assessment. First, consider the potential partner's existing partners. Are any of them your competitors? Do they replicate or complement the assets and capabilities that you bring to the table? Second, gauge the potential partner's level of interest in your assets and capabilities. From their perspective, how useful is your customer base? To what degree can your data sets and value propositions help them to improve their service offerings? Third, consider how willing the partner is to collaborate on a longer timeframe, based on their track record of established partnerships and strategic priorities. Do they share your vision for deep collaboration and creating value together? Finally, consider whether the potential partner has the capacity to move rapidly from discussion to implementation of the partnerships. Are they as committed as you are to nurturing the partnership and helping it to thrive?

As you make your way through the list of potential ecosystem partners from your partnership matrix, think about how each player would satisfy these criteria. From there, you can narrow the list down even more and prioritize who to approach first. The goal, of course, is to find partners who truly share your vision, who have what you need to achieve it, and who are an ideal fit for the new ecosystem you are imagining.

EXAMPLE 1: HOME

Of course, it's one thing to discuss all of this in the abstract—it's quite another to see it in practice. To give you a deeper sense of what we're talking about here, let's explore these questions through the lens of a few examples. We can begin with one that will already be familiar: the example of a player in the home space that we discussed in Chapter 4.

You will recall that we imagined a generic player in the home space—perhaps an HVAC equipment supplier, perhaps a software or cloud player, or perhaps even a gas or electricity utility. We further imagined that this player was interested in offering a proposition that we call "comfort and security as a service"—in other words, a service in which customers pay a recurring fee, and in return, are guaranteed that parameters such as temperature and humidity will be kept within a certain range at all times within their home and that the premises will be monitored and kept secure. In the previous chapter, we covered how a few different existing home players might weigh this proposition by looking at their evolving customer base and customer needs, assessing the ecosystem landscape, determining if an ecosystem is needed, and then assessing the competitive landscape.

Now let's continue the story, and consider how such a home player might go about choosing a role and picking ecosystem partners. Say, for example, that you are an HVAC equipment manufacturer wanting to make this comfort-and-security-as-a-service proposition. The first order of business is deciding what role to play. In other words, will you be the one to bring this new ecosystem together? Or will you need to seek out an ecosystem orchestrated by someone else? However, as we previously explained, this choice involves more than just picking from two possibilities—rather, it's a matter of identifying where you belong on a spectrum of options. Assuming you have the ambition to orchestrate, begin by asking yourself some key questions: How well would your past experience serve you as an orchestrator? Can you really offer more value for your customers and for others in the ecosystem as an orchestrator than you could as a participant?

Next, you would begin your ecosystem necessities analysis. Ask yourself: What assets or capabilities do you need to be successful in this comfort-and-safety-as-a-service proposition? For example, you would need the capability to assemble and distribute the necessary HVAC equipment, security cameras, and other physical infrastructure. This, fortunately, may be a capability you already possess as an equipment manufacturer. But chances are that such a player would lack at least a few other critical capabilities. For instance, you would need the ability to install and maintain that equipment, which may go beyond the scope of your current operation. Perhaps most importantly, you would need an online platform to connect all the devices, sensors, and other equipment—allowing for the creation of digital twins for real-time remote digital monitoring. This online platform would also allow customers to make adjustments, access camera footage, and manage their subscription, all in one place. A cloud or software player, by contrast, would begin with strong platform-building capabilities, but would lack the capabilities to build and distribute HVAC equipment.

Whatever your situation, at this point, you will have generated a list of all the assets and capabilities needed to make your offer a reality. What you need to do next is to give some structure to your list, and begin using it to plan your path forward. The best way to do this is with the ecosystem necessities analysis matrix. The assets and capabilities filled into the matrix shown in Figure 5.7 are a hypothetical sample to demonstrate how this might look for a player crafting a comfort-and-safety-as-a-service proposition.

Once you've put this critical list of necessary capabilities together in your matrix, take a hard look at yourself and ask if you possess them today—or if you are on a path to possessing them in the future. It's

FIGURE 5.7 **Ecosystem necessities analysis (Home example)**

Platform

	POSITION TODAY:		POSITION IN THE FUTURE:	
	YOURS	COMPETITION'S	YOURS	COMPETITION'S
• Connect all the safety and comfort devices to collect data • Monitor and control the key parameters • Build intelligence to modify the parameters with algorithms based on the data collected • Leverage the platform for third-party players to build offers for customers in the ecosystem • Sell both your own offers and third-party offers • Bill and collect fees for the services offered by everyone in the ecosystem • Build digital twins				

Go-to-Market capabilities

	POSITION TODAY:		POSITION IN THE FUTURE:	
	YOURS	COMPETITION'S	YOURS	COMPETITION'S
• Physical and digital partnerships to drive sales • Channels and sales forces owned and controlled by you • Channel support for pre- and post-sale				

Customers

	POSITION TODAY:		POSITION IN THE FUTURE:	
	YOURS	COMPETITION'S	YOURS	COMPETITION'S
• Equipment installation • Equipment maintenance and repair • Ongoing customer services to ensure satisfaction				

important not to flatter yourself here—the goal of this process is not to celebrate your accomplishments, but to arrive at a clear-eyed assessment of what changes are necessary to achieve your vision, and ultimately to determine what role you should be playing. If the answer is no, you need to determine how you can get them. Again, there are several ways of doing this. You could try to develop them on your own internally. You could acquire an outside company that already has them. Or you could establish an ecosystem partnership.

To decide which of these options is most appropriate for each asset or capability, consider the relative difficulty of developing and maintaining them. Some assets or capabilities may be easy to develop and easy to maintain. If you're a software or cloud player, building a digital platform for the comfort-and-safety-as-a-service proposition probably fits squarely within your wheelhouse. And with teams of talented developers who are deeply experienced with such systems, maintaining the platform is also less likely to be difficult. This is a situation in which building the capability internally on your own is clearly the favorable option. But imagine again, for a moment, that you are an HVAC equipment manufacturer. In this case, building a sophisticated cloud-based online platform may be a tall order, indeed, as would maintaining it. (On the other hand, it might not be.) If it is, however, then given those difficulties, an ecosystem partnership would be a much more effective way of obtaining digital platform capabilities.

By sorting your desired assets and capabilities into your build, acquire, or partner grid, you will begin to get more of a sense of where you belong on the spectrum between orchestrator and participant. If most of the structural capabilities of organizing, distribution, and go-to-market are landing in the bottom-right corner of the organizer, that may be a sign that you are better off as a participant—or at least in a role on the participant side of the spectrum. If those capabilities are landing on the upper- or lower-right quadrants, and more peripheral capabilities are landing in the lower-right, that would be an indication that you are better situated to orchestrate. If the most significant, structural capabilities are falling evenly across the organizer, or are falling in no discernable pattern, that is a sign that you are perhaps best suited for a hybrid role, somewhere in the middle of the spectrum. If so, determining where exactly you belong and what exactly that role looks like will require careful attention to detail, several more iterations of the capability assessment process—and some judgment calls.

Once you have determined which assets and capabilities to develop on your own, and which need to be obtained by way of an ecosystem, the next step is to begin scouting out and assessing potential partners. Begin with the list of assets and capabilities that you sorted into the lower-right quadrant of your build, acquire, or partner grid—that is, those assets and capabilities that are best suited to obtaining through an ecosystem partnership. As you enter these assets and capabilities into your partnership matrix, consider which collaborators could potentially provide them for your ecosystem. For instance, if you are an HVAC manufacturer, a cloud-based platform would probably fall in the lower-right quadrant of your build, acquire, or partner grid—so it would make sense to begin thinking about which cloud-based tech players could do a good job of building such a platform for your ecosystem.

Once your partnership matrix is complete, you can begin narrowing your options down to a shortlist by evaluating the different potential collaborators in terms of the two broad categories of criteria that we mentioned earlier—attractiveness and feasibility. For example, if you are an HVAC equipment manufacturer, an online or software player would be an ideal choice as they would be well positioned to fill in the missing but critical capability of building the platform. They are an *attractive* potential collaborator. (Though, it is important to note that in such a scenario, partnering with an online player carries a risk of putting that player in a position to disintermediate you—so you would be wise to proceed with caution.) At the same time, you bring something important to the table, too: your equipment, which is essential to the value proposition. This makes the partnership *feasible*. Once you have formed your shortlist of potential collaborators, you will want to repeat the whole process several times, cycling back and forth through the various components as shown in Figure 5.2 on p. 138 until you are confident that you have identified the most promising candidates.

EXAMPLE 2: PAYMENT FINTECH

Continuing on, let's consider how we might tackle these questions in a slightly different context. Let's say you are a company working in the financial technology (or fintech) space. Imagine that you are either a fintech company that offers a payment function or a bank with payment capabilities. And let's further suppose that by going through the process that we laid out in the previous chapter, you have already decided that you need to differentiate yourself—to expand beyond payments and offer a value proposition that includes e-commerce, as well. By e-commerce, we mean functionality for an online marketplace in which customers and merchants can buy and sell things on a platform that builds off of your payments infrastructure. To do this, you have determined that you need an ecosystem.

The first thing to do is to choose what role you will play in the new ecosystem. The more ambitious choice, of course, would be to orchestrate—to bring in a variety of different ecosystem partners around your own platform in order to facilitate the e-commerce value proposition, and ultimately make life more convenient for your customers. But you may find that you lack the capabilities or resources to marshal such a group of participants around your value proposition. You may find that it is a better choice to simply partner with one of these players and collaboratively build a platform together. In which case you would perhaps not be the orchestrator, but still more than a plain old participant. You would, after all, be supplying critical technology on which the rest of the ecosystem would rely. On the other hand, you could opt to be a plain old participant—you could identify one of the early e-commerce platforms, and come in as a critical differentiated supplier, offering your payments system to the other players on that existing platform.

But let us suppose, for the moment, that you aspire to orchestrate the combined payments and e-commerce ecosystem you are imagining. The next step is to undertake an ecosystem necessities analysis—in other words, begin thinking about what capabilities you would need to orchestrate. First and foremost, you would need a digital platform, which would allow you to bring together your payment services with e-commerce, and (if desired) numerous other adjacent add-on services, like a loyalty points program, gamified peer-to-peer payments (a payments capability integrated with chat or other social apps), B2B services (like accounting, legal, and HR), and more. Given your starting position as a payments fintech player, chances are you will already possess a platform of some kind, but it may not have all of the elements you need to offer this new value proposition—you may need to modify, improve, or expand upon it. What other assets or capabilities would you need? The ability to attract, sign up, and retain customers—which is to say, marketing, promotion, distribution channels, supply chain, forward and backward logistics, and more.

Some of these may be easier than others to build and/or maintain on your own. Imagine plotting them into a build, acquire, or partner matrix. As we mentioned, you probably would already have a platform, so you would have a relatively easy time building an e-commerce platform by modifying or adding to your existing one. Distribution channels, supply chain, and logistics, on the other hand, are a different story. It would be an incredibly complex and arduous process to try to build these capabilities yourself—to set up and organize a warehouse, figure out shipping, returns, and everything else. And maintaining them would be even more difficult. For all of these reasons, your best option would be to obtain these capabilities through an ecosystem partnership, by bringing outside players into a shared-value-creation relationship.

Next, after you have determined which assets and capabilities you will need to obtain through ecosystem partnerships, figure out which players are best positioned to provide them. Survey the landscape, looking at all the players (whether they are currently in your sector or not) who currently possess those capabilities or could conceivably develop them in the future. Consider which are the most attractive to you—which ones, for example, might provide not only a much-needed capability but a strong customer base, too? Then consider which ones will have the strongest incentives to want to work with you and join your ecosystem as a participant.

EXAMPLE 3: HEALTH

We will end the chapter by considering what role to play and which partners to choose through a somewhat different lens. Imagine that you are a company that works within the health space or wants to move into it—perhaps an insurance company, or a medical device manufacturer, or a cloud or software player. By following the process that we laid out in Chapter 4, you would have already decided where to play and how to evolve your value proposition to account for your changing customer needs and customer base. Let us imagine that you have decided to pursue a proposition of integrated health and wellness services—a hub through which customers can find solutions to all of their health and wellness needs. This would include not only functions like finding a doctor, tracking vital signs, getting personalized treatment (based on genetic information), and managing insurance claims—but also finding exercise classes, tracking fitness and diet regimens, and managing mental health. With the proposition identified, let us also suppose that you have determined you will need an ecosystem to pull it off—meaning you will either need to build one or you will need to join one. Now the question before you is: What role should you assume within this ecosystem? To what degree can you—or do you want to—be in charge of the ecosystem? Where on the spectrum from orchestrator to participant should you fall?

First, decide whether you have the ambition to orchestrate. As we previously discussed, this is a difficult decision, which rests in large part on your existing and future potential capabilities. But successfully doing so carries with it the promise of not only finding a high degree of monetary success, but also making a meaningful difference in people's lives. Given all of that, you need to ask yourself honestly: Can you really offer more value for your customers as an ecosystem orchestrator than you could by participating in someone else's ecosystem?

Next, perform an ecosystem necessities analysis. Start by considering all of the different assets and capabilities that will be needed to pull off your proposition. Chances are your desired proposition will require a digital platform to integrate all of the different health and wellness services you will offer. You will need a way to attract, sign up, and retain customers. You will need networks of doctors and insurance companies as well as wellness and fitness providers. And you will need ongoing customer service, marketing, promotion, and more. Now the question is: Which of these assets and capabilities do you already have? And which will you need to obtain?

For example, if you are a health insurance company, you may already have the capacity to help customers navigate claims, and you probably have strong connections to medical practitioners like doctors and other specialists. However, you may lack the sort of large-scale, customer-facing digital platform that would be necessary to bring your desired proposition together. You may also have to worry about regulatory requirements. On the other hand, if you are a cloud or software player, creating such a platform would be much easier, but you might lack other assets or capabilities, like the ability to navigate medical bureaucracy or regulatory regimes—or the ability to record and keep track of your customers' vital signs. As you think through these necessary assets and capabilities, you can systematize your thinking by leveraging an ecosystem necessities analysis matrix.

From there, you can then place the assets and capabilities into a build, acquire, or partner grid to determine which capabilities should be developed internally, which should be obtained by acquisition, and which should be obtained through ecosystem partnerships. To decide which path is best for each asset or capability, evaluate it based on how difficult it would be to develop and maintain. As we covered earlier in the chapter, the assets and capabilities that land in the lower-right quadrant of the grid—that is, difficult to develop and difficult to maintain—are those that will be best suited to obtaining through ecosystem partnerships. So, again, if you are a health insurance company, the digital platform you will need in order to bring together your ecosystem would likely fall into this category. If you are a cloud or software player, you might want to bring in a network of doctors as ecosystem partners.

Once you've completed your build, acquire, or partner grid, it is time to choose which collaborators can most effectively help bring your ecosystem to completion. To start narrowing in on exactly what partners you will need, and to begin conceptualizing how you will prioritize them, think about potential gives and gets—what types of business models you should use to structure the relationship between you and your collaborators. Next, leverage your partnership matrix to determine which potential collaborators are well positioned to provide the assets and capabilities you need. If you are a cloud or software player, for example, you may need capabilities such as medical device technology (for gathering and monitoring key vital signs and other necessary health parameters), insurance, and fitness tracking—so some of the players that show up on your partnership matrix may include insurance companies, hospitals, fitness tracking companies, and medical device manufacturers. If you are an insurance company, on the other hand, chances are very high that you will need a digital platform, and thus your partnership matrix is likely to include cloud or software companies.

Finally, once you have finished your partnership matrix, you can begin a process of narrowing down the different potential collaborators to a shortlist, by assessing their attractiveness and the feasibility of the match: Do they want to partner with you? And do you want to partner with them?

We hope by now that the power of partnerships in forming strong ecosystems has become clear. Bringing other players into the fold and creating value with them collaboratively gives you the power to build much more than you ever could on your own—even if you are coming from a position of immense power and influence. Ultimately, ecosystems are about building community and bringing different parties with different interests together—in the true spirit of serving customers' best interests.

Once you have decided how to evolve your proposition, chosen where to play, picked your role, and chosen partners, the only thing left to do is to transform your organization from within to sustain and build upon the changes you are planning. This means rethinking every aspect of how you work: your organizational and operating models, your approach to talent, your performance management style, your culture building, and your supporting infrastructure. All of this is what we will cover in the next chapter.

THINGS TO WATCH OUT FOR WHEN CHOOSING A ROLE AND EVALUATING PARTNERS

1. **Lacking clarity about what "partnership" really means:** As we've mentioned earlier, many companies recognize the importance of ecosystem partnerships, and genuinely want to take steps to build them, but suffer from a lack of clarity about what that means, and the depth of commitment that is involved. They think they can simply take what they are currently doing and call it by a different name. Hence, many businesses will tout "partnerships" that are, in fact, one-dimensional vendor or customer relationships—even in cases that involve a significant Requisition for Proposal (RFP) type process that pits vendors against one another. Real ecosystem relationships are vastly more complicated and constantly evolving; they involve joint value creation, integrated teams, and so on. Again, there's nothing inherently wrong with calling your existing customer and vendor relationships "partnerships," but doing so distracts you from the more meaningful task of building deeper, comprehensive ecosystems that will set you up for success in the future.

2. **Placing too much emphasis on your starting position:** When beginning to think about ecosystems, many companies, understandably, are heavily influenced by their existing organization and the sector in which they have traditionally worked. This can push you toward faulty conclusions when considering what role to take, or which partners to choose. Frequently, companies that make this mistake suffer from a lack of ambition, becoming overfocused on where they have the "right to play" or on how to build on legacy strengths rather than developing new ones. Instead, they would do much better to focus their energies on finding imaginative possibilities for using ecosystems to expand their reach.

3. **Overestimating your ability to orchestrate:** Almost everyone tends to think they're better than everyone else, even when there's scant evidence to support that belief.

We all fall victim to this trap. In psychology, it is known as illusory superiority, a cognitive bias that pushes us to ignore or minimize our shortcomings, and to overestimate our competence.[3] This shows up, for example, in the fact that an overwhelming majority of American drivers, roughly three quarters, rate themselves as above-average drivers.[4] The world of ecosystems would be no exception to this phenomenon. If you overestimate your ability to orchestrate, this can cause you not only to miss out on the benefits that proper attention to the ecosystem economy could bring, but actively wastes your time by misdirecting your attention to endeavors that will likely never come to fruition.

4. **Getting caught up in red tape:** Especially when larger and more established companies become interested in building ecosystems, we tend to see players get bogged down in an overly-complex administrative process. When bringing new partners on board, you want to avoid having to go through numerous committees, meetings, legal reviews, and other steps. You need to be able to move fast and develop a dynamic, agile process. Making it as easy and as seamless as possible will help keep everyone involved feeling motivated and satisfied that they have entered into a fair arrangement.

6

Survival of the Fittest— Changing from the Inside Out

How to Make the Leap

In the previous two chapters, we provided you with some practical ways of planning how to leverage the emerging ecosystem economy to your advantage—whether that means building a new ecosystem yourself, participating in someone else's ecosystem, or somewhere in between. But this is only half of the equation. Deciding where to play, evolving your proposition, choosing what role to play, and who to partner with—these steps will only get you so far. To truly make the leap and find success in the new world of ecosystems, you need to effect change from within. You need to transform your organization from the inside out.

As we've said before, when it comes to building ecosystem businesses, half-measures are unlikely to do much good. Making a series of halfhearted, superficial changes will not cut it—in fact, doing so will hurt your chances by wasting precious time. Tinkering around the edges will not help, either. You need to rethink your approach on a fundamental level. So, to help you process the task, we've broken down the key elements you need to focus on into five discrete categories: organizational and operating model, talent, performance management, underlying culture, and supporting infrastructure.

While the advice in the following pages may seem most applicable to orchestrators, we should stipulate that much of it could be equally applicable to participants, and even companies that are not proactively leveraging the ecosystem economy. After all, not all companies will want, or need, to embark on an ecosystem journey. While each of the five categories we just listed is of vital importance, they do not represent a sequential process that needs to be followed in a specific order. You can approach these issues in whatever order makes sense for you as you work to build a successful ecosystem business. In the ecosystem economy, businesses will face an array of daunting new challenges: competition from unexpected sources, the erosion of long-standing incumbent advantages, and an increasingly unpredictable environment. To get ahead, companies will need a comprehensive approach that involves fundamental, meaningful changes in all of these areas.

ORGANIZATIONAL AND OPERATING MODEL

One of the hardest parts of rising to the demands of the new ecosystem economy is the task of building an ecosystem-oriented business within an organizational framework that is simply not set up to do so. To successfully build ecosystem-oriented businesses, then, you will need to devise a new organizational model. This clearly is no small task, but as we've stressed several times already, taking advantage of the emerging ecosystem economy is an endeavor that requires deep, fundamental changes. Given how important this is, the work of building an ecosystem-oriented business has to be at the top of the agenda for the CEO, senior management, and the board.

But in addition to being a higher priority for senior management, ecosystems need to shape your organizational model in other ways, too. For instance, you will need to think carefully about how the ecosystem businesses you are contemplating will fit into your organizational model and governance structure. Our research shows that the vast majority of unsuccessful ecosystem builds can trace their failure back to a flawed approach to governance. This is understandable because organizational structures designed for businesses in traditional sectors are ill-suited for ecosystem businesses that cut across sectors.

There are two types of governance that we need to worry about. One is the work of deciding where you put the ecosystem business within your broader business. The second is deciding how to govern the ecosystem itself—how do you determine who gets what? How do you grapple with security issues and development issues? If others are contributing to the ecosystem, how will they be compensated beyond traditional value-sharing arrangements? How will you police your ecosystem to make sure partners and participants are not taking advantage of the ecosystem and doing things that would harm others? In weighing all these questions, perhaps what is most important is being thoughtful and purposeful in deciding on a set of guiding principles—and then making those principles transparent and evolving them to make sure there is an equitable position for everyone involved.

Depending on your starting point, your level of ambition, and a number of other factors, you will have a range of different options as to where your cross-sectoral ecosystem business will reside within your larger organization. We can think of these options as fitting onto a spectrum. One end represents scenarios in which your ecosystem businesses fit squarely within your existing core business—in such a case, you may be able to fit the ecosystem business into an organizational model designed for businesses in traditional sectors (as an integrated unit with a distinct structure). The other end of the spectrum are scenarios in which your ecosystem businesses are more like "moonshots," separate from your existing core business in traditional sectors. In that case, you may need more independent structures of the kind that are frequently employed in classic investment setups or development labs—which will help you attract the right talent and create the required focus. Most new ecosystem business builds fall in between these two ends of the spectrum.

Where you land on this spectrum will determine how effectively you can foster an entrepreneurial spirit while balancing your ability to leverage existing capabilities to scale up new propositions. Landing too far toward one extreme or the other can cause serious problems—and, in fact, this is one of the top reasons why some ecosystems falter. If you keep them too close to the core organization, their innovative, entrepreneurial spirit will be stifled. But keep them too far away, and they will struggle to scale up and benefit from synergies. Organizations, therefore, must strive to find a "Goldilocks zone" for most of their ecosystem businesses, at least until they successfully scale up and become fully independent. That is, they must develop ecosystem ideas that are not too close to the core business, but also not too far.

Many incumbents have devised clever ways to ensure that they are able to consistently find this Goldilocks zone. Some businesses have formed internal incubators or accelerators, which operate at the edges of the existing core organization, aiming to have the best of both worlds. These internal incubators or accelerators usually provide a place for entrepreneurial talent with more freedom than what existing core business unit organizations can offer, while also maintaining healthy connections to those units. This makes them ideally positioned to foster innovation, but if they are to build true ecosystem businesses, they need to do more still—that is to say, they need to develop ecosystem-enabled capabilities. These include, among other things: leadership with a cross-industrial perspective and experience (to evaluate ideas and manage them through their lifecycle with a stage-gated approach); strong core partnership capabilities (to develop, foster, and sustain a large number of complex ecosystem partnerships); highlynetworked HR functions to attract and retain cross-sectoral talent; independent IT to enable high-speed, startup-like development into entirely new business sectors; and clear connections, or bridges, to the existing core business units (e.g., talent rotation between the new ecosystem business and the existing core business, with key oversight roles filled by existing core business unit leaders). Depending on where you are on the spectrum we described above, we expect that as you mature and scale up your ecosystem-based businesses, you will likely benefit from migrating your organizational model to an integrated model in which ecosystem-based businesses become the core of your organization (in which case, the line of demarcation between the existing core business and new ecosystem businesses would fade away). This is especially important as the ecosystem economy represents a larger and larger portion of the broader economy.

These ecosystem incubator organizations also need to be skilled at managing the lifecycle of new business ideas, which in many cases means having highly adaptable teams that can build and test prototypes supervised by a set of portfolio managers. In the event that an ecosystem business takes off, there needs to be a path for these ideas to graduate to a more independent status, in which case they would have their own boards, CEOs, and management teams. Naturally, each of these businesses would need to deliver on their key performance indicators (KPIs) or face closure, in the spirit of failing fast.

No matter where you fall on the spectrum with your ecosystem business, you need new ways of working and new models of collaboration to get things done. The ecosystem economy demands an organizational structure that is nimble, fast moving, and adaptable. One area from which we can take some inspiration here is the practice of so-called agile management. This concept was originally exclusive to software development and traces its roots back to an influential document published in 2001 called the "Manifesto for Agile Software Development," written by a group of seventeen developers during a ski retreat in Utah. They were interested in finding alternatives to the so-called heavyweight software development processes that were dominant at the time, and which they felt were bogged down by cumbersome procedures, bureaucracy, and busywork.[1] Their proposed solution was a method that favored rapid, iterative development carried out by dynamic, self-organizing, heterogeneous teams, working non-hierarchically. The traditional heavyweight model of software development (also known as a waterfall model) emphasized a slow, painstakingly careful method that sought to include everything and meet every client need, all together as part of a single, drawn-out cycle of development (see Figure 6.1).

The agile approach, by contrast, sought to quickly address *just the core needs* of the clients, and then continually evolve the product based on their feedback and usage patterns. In the world of IT and software development, this model found resounding success and over the course of several years became widely adopted. With the agile model, developers found they could boost their productivity, do their work faster and with fewer schedule overruns, and ultimately deliver a more stable and higher-quality product to their clients.

In the wake of such success, the principles of this movement soon extended far beyond the world of software development. Over the next fifteen years or so, companies began to use the principles of the agile model to shape their strategy around a wider range of technologies and products—not just software. Before long, business leaders started applying the core agile principles to the way they structured and operated their companies as well. After all, the problems implicit in the old, slow-moving, waterfall model of software development were also in many cases endemic within the bureaucratic organizational structure of businesses. It only made sense that the prescription would be the same. As Stephen Denning, author of a book called *The Age of Agile*, explained in *Forbes*, "Agile's emergence as a huge global movement extending beyond software is driven by the discovery that the only way for organizations to cope with today's turbulent

FIGURE 6.1 **Illustration of traditional vs. agile models**

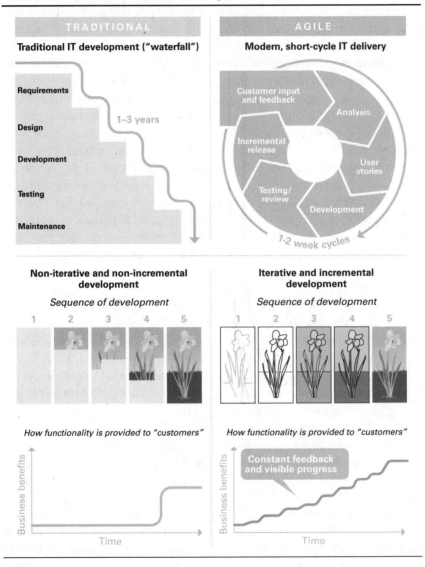

customer-driven marketplace is to become agile. Agile enables organizations to master continuous change. It permits firms to flourish in a world that is increasingly volatile, uncertain, complex and ambiguous"—in other words, in exactly the sort of conditions that characterize the new ecosystem economy.[2]

Extending agile principles to your organizational structure means transforming your company from a top-down, hierarchical, bureaucratic, machine model to an adaptive, flexible, cooperative, organic model. In the old model, a leadership team would give directives to a middle-management layer, which then filtered those directions down to siloed teams of workers and attempted to arbitrate between them and coordinate their efforts in order to meet a deadline or some other target. This was a model that introduced inefficiencies at every turn: rigid, inflexible, and fastidious to a fault. Poor communication among different levels of management and different teams of specialists created friction and resulted in these groups essentially creating work for one another. In short, it was impossible to fail fast—which is a key characteristic that's needed in the new ecosystem economy.

The agile model, on the other hand, is all about failing fast. In the agile model, the inefficient bureaucracy is cut out, and leadership directly supervises a range of dynamic, heterogeneous teams.

Agile is an ideal organizational response to the emerging ecosystem economy, not only because it addresses the surface effects of that shift—the increasingly unpredictable competitive environment, the changing customer needs, and the constant introduction of disruptive technology—but also because its underlying principles reflect the way that ecosystems work. Consider some of the trademarks of agile organizations. They are composed of various tribes, or business groups, which in turn are composed of members from different competency groups, or chapters, which are divided into a network of small, high-performance, cross-functional teams, often called squads (see Figure 6.3). Agile organizations work in rapid, iterative cycles of innovation, impact, and learning. They excel by connecting the dots between different team members' skillsets to get things done—and by empowering employees to take full ownership. And, finally, they leverage the latest technology to find new ways of unlocking value and evolving their business. All of these trademarks are highly relevant in building an ecosystem business. Essentially what you need to do is to reflect the fundamental values and practices of ecosystems within your own organization.

Finally, in addition to changing your organizational model, you will also need to rethink your operating model. That is to say, not just the framework that structures your business, but also the way you and your team work together within that framework to get things done.

FIGURE 6.2   **Comparison of traditional organization model vs. agile organization model**

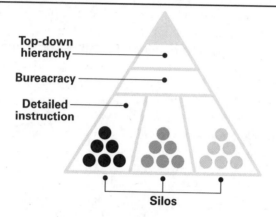

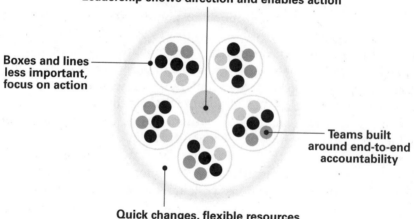

This concept of the operating model can involve many of the elements that we will discuss in other sections of this chapter, including how you and your team communicate, how you hold each other accountable, how you review performance, how you handle consequence management, and how you reward team members and help them to grow and develop. In other words, what are the practical and tactical ways you and your team work together to accomplish the tasks in front of you? This, too, will need to be substantially rethought in order to build successful ecosystem businesses.

FIGURE 6.3 **Business agile team examples: Tribes, squads, and chapters**

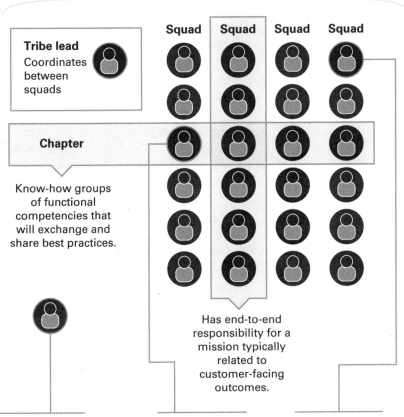

Tribe
Integrates several thematically connected squads with no more than 150 people.

Tribe lead
Coordinates between squads

Squad Squad Squad Squad

Chapter

Know-how groups of functional competencies that will exchange and share best practices.

Has end-to-end responsibility for a mission typically related to customer-facing outcomes.

Agile coach
- Focuses on individual and team coaching
- Flags impediments at team and system level

Chapter leader
- Responsible for growing and developing competencies for chapter members

Product Owner
- Prioritizes activities of squad
- Maintains backlog and to-do list of squad
- Unlike classic manager, takes approach of servant leadership

TALENT

Evolving your organizational and operating models will go a long way toward helping you adapt to the new ecosystem economy—but it won't get you all the way there. You will also need the right talent. In fact, talent is one of the critical ingredients to evolving your organizational and operating models. You might think about the task of transforming your organization as you would the task of building a house. Implementing an effective agile model is absolutely essential. It is like the wood frame that hold the house up—the studs, trusses, joists, bracing, and rafters. But if that frame is all you have, the house can't serve its purpose of providing shelter and security. For that, you need to fill in the frame with siding, insulation, wall board, flooring, a roof, electrical wiring, plumbing, and so much more.

Similarly, your new organizational model will not be able to serve its purpose unless it is populated by the right kind of talent. Finding quality talent is getting tougher and tougher—and the gig economy is only exacerbating the difficulty. There are hundreds, possibly thousands, of different methods and theories on how to identify the right people for your organization. You will likely find a whole shelf of books at your local bookstore expounding these different philosophies. Succeeding in the world of ecosystems, however, requires a special set of qualities and abilities. This means you will need to do more than just finding people who are highly skilled, with excellent critical thinking skills, who have years of solid experience, and who have found a high degree of success in past jobs. We can sort the qualities you need to look for into three different buckets: diversity (of experience, thought, and background); openness to new ideas; and a predisposition to deep collaboration.

We begin with diversity. Of course, there are different kinds of diversity, and you want all of them to be reflected in your business. For instance, there is diversity of experience—meaning a variety of different professional and personal experiences. There is diversity of thought—meaning a variety of different intellectual temperaments. And then there is diversity of background—meaning people who come from different places, who were brought up in different ways and according to different cultural or religious traditions.

Take diversity of experience, for example. In our professional lives, all of us have encountered colleagues or employees who embody the two ends of the spectrum. On the one hand, there is the hyper-specialist, the person who ignores other potential interests and opportunities to doggedly focus on one narrow, specific area, but is deeply knowledgeable—brilliant, even—when it comes to that area. On the other hand, there is the inquisitive generalist, always learning a new skill, reading up on some new area of the business, or organizing some new initiative, but never going deep. Both of these archetypes come with their upsides and downsides, but the generalists by far have the poorer reputation. Hyper-specialists tend to be romanticized, and viewed as intense, passionate experts, while the generalists are written off as unserious dabblers. But in the context of ecosystems, it can actually be *good* to be a dabbler—to have limited experience in a wide variety of fields, rather than deep experience in one.

This is what we mean when we call a person well-rounded—and it is the rationale behind the liberal arts tradition in education, which dates back to ancient Greece.[3] A wide variety of experience helps us to develop a deeper and more effective way of engaging with the world around us, which can lead to all sorts of advantages, both in our work and in our personal lives. This idea was the focus of a 2019 book by the journalist David Epstein called *Range: Why Generalists Triumph in a Specialized World*. In it, Epstein explores why people in many different areas, from sports to creative pursuits to the world of business, are more successful when they take a circuitous route to finding their calling, or when they explore a more diverse set of life experiences, rather than fixating on and training toward a narrow goal beginning from a very early age. For example, an athlete who has played a variety of different sports and accumulated a balanced set of athletic skills may end up being more effective than one who has trained for a specific position in a single sport from childhood. Similarly, an artist who has explored different forms of creative expression in music, dance, painting, and sculpture may ultimately find more inspiration and creative energy than one who has pursued a single discipline with focused intensity.

In other words, our success isn't necessarily determined by the highly specific, painstakingly developed skills we use every day in the narrow confines of our professions—rather, it is a product of more general, meta-level skills that we develop as we acquire a wide breadth of experience. Succeeding is more about learning to learn than it is about learning specific things. The problem is that the world pushes us in the opposite direction. As Epstein puts it, "the challenge we all face is how to maintain the benefits of breadth, diverse experience, interdisciplinary thinking, and delayed concentration in a world that increasingly incentivizes, even demands, hyperspecialization." We can all do better, he suggests, if only we can learn to stick our heads outside of the specialized niches we've found and cultivate a broader set of knowledge.[4]

Consider, for example, a story from Steve Jobs's early days that shows the importance of this sort of diversity of experience. In 1973, Jobs had dropped out of Reed College in Portland, Oregon. He had yet to embark on his journeys through India and was still several years away from founding Apple in 1976. Bored and short on money, Jobs was still hanging around the Reed College campus and decided to audit a course in calligraphy—that is, he sat in on the class even though it wouldn't count toward a degree, just for the pleasure of learning about a new topic. The course was taught by a former Roman Catholic priest, Robert Palladino, who had honed his craft in a monastic order and was widely considered to be one of the world's foremost practitioners of calligraphy. According to a 2005 commencement address that Jobs gave at Stanford University, the experience of auditing the calligraphy course inspired him to pay close attention, years later, to the onscreen typography of Apple's new computers, and ultimately bore a great influence on the company's widely celebrated design philosophy.[5] "I learned about serif and sans serif typefaces, about varying the amount of space between different letter combinations, about what makes great typography great," Jobs recalled. "It was beautiful, historical, artistically subtle in a way that science can't capture, and I found it fascinating. . . . Ten years later, when we were designing the first Macintosh computer, it all came back to me. And we designed it all into the Mac. It was the first computer with beautiful typography. If I had never dropped in on that single course in college, the Mac would have never had multiple typefaces or proportionally spaced fonts."[6]

This perfectly captures the sort of diversity of experience that companies need to be looking for today when evaluating potential new talent in the context of the ecosystem economy. At so many companies, and more broadly within the corporate world today, the hiring process is structurally biased toward those who specialize in one area—and against generalists, those working between disciplines, or those, like Jobs, who have gone out of their way to seek out new experiences just for the pleasure of learning. We tend to think of openings narrowly, as fitting into a single category. And we have difficulty figuring out how to incorporate the skills and contributions of a person with multiple kinds of experience. Headhunting practices and AI recruitment tools can reinforce these biases. The algorithms that so often evaluate resumes and candidates sometimes favor those who have the most experience in a single area, rather than those who have learned about the workings of many different businesses and sectors. In the ecosystem economy, where the name of the game is finding creative new ways to interlink the workings of previously discrete sectors, we should be actively seeking out candidates who have this sort of multiplicity of experience.

Of course, this is not to say that specialists are unimportant—or that they should be any less valued in a company that is looking to adapt to the demands of the ecosystem economy. Building a successful ecosystem business requires both specialists and generalists. But in many instances, our current practices and incentives lead us to be biased against generalists and toward specialists, so we need to be especially attentive to making sure that we include the perspectives of generalists.

Diversity of experience, however, isn't the only kind of diversity that is needed. To truly get ahead in the ecosystem economy, you need diversity of thought and diversity of background, too. You need people who not only have different professional and life experiences, but people who think differently and who have different backgrounds and values and upbringings. Prioritizing these factors will lead to a team that is better at seeing and judging the world around them—that better understands the motivations of different groups and that can better predict how different kinds of people will react to a given situation.

Consider Jeff Bezos, for example, who spent long hours as a child tinkering with and repairing tractors and other equipment on his grandparents' ranch in Texas. According to a profile in *Fortune*, Bezos felt that the experience inspired in him a passion for experimentation—a passion that might not have been activated had he come with a different background. "Experiments are key to innovation because they rarely turn out as you expect and you learn so much," Bezos explained. At Amazon, he continued, he and his team were trying "to reduce the cost of doing experiments so that we can do more of them. If you can increase the number of experiments you try from a hundred to a thousand, you dramatically increase the number of innovations you produce."[7]

Another crucial element of adapting your talent to the demands of the ecosystem economy is finding people who are open to new ideas. This is distinct from, but closely related to the need for a diversity of experience, thought, and background. After all, those who are curious and open to the world around them will naturally acquire a more diverse set of professional experiences—and thus a deeply varied and wide-ranging reserve of skills, knowledge, and understanding. But while it is certainly important to cultivate a variety of different kinds of professional experience, it is just as important for employees to seek out new ideas and new forms of knowledge in the broader world. That is, it is important for employees to have hobbies, to cultivate niche interests, and to pursue knowledge for its own sake.

As a business navigating the ecosystem economy, you want to seek out employees who are open to unexpected ideas and unconventional forms of knowledge. For it is these employees who will have the creativity, the foresight, and the powers of abstract thinking needed to fuse previously separate value propositions into visionary new combinations that will create value and help you grow your business. Again, this is not to say that you should aim for uniformity in any respect. You do not need to find a full team of people who all have the same skills and characteristics. As we mentioned already, the goal is to achieve a diverse mix of different kinds of people and different profiles of talent.

Finally, the last element of evolving your approach to talent is seeking out people who are predisposed to collaboration. Unfortunately, it is quite common—especially in large organizations with traditional, hierarchical structures—for people to become territorial and thus fixated on their own achievements and progress over the collective objectives of the team. Certain organizational models can reinforce these dynamics—as opposed to an agile model, which builds upon collaboration as the foundational bedrock. In addition to the agile model, seeking out talent who are predisposed to collaboration can help reverse the phenomenon of territorialism by focusing team members instead on a common goal—on building something together. In the ecosystem economy, you need your business to be populated by employees who have the bravery to step outside of their comfort zone and forge cross-departmental and cross-sectoral connections. After all, these connections are the true essence of a successful ecosystem play. You also need the kind of collaborative approach that will naturally speed your development cycle and foster a fast-fail mindset (more on this later in the chapter). With enough encouragement, all of this together can begin to create a new, positive environment of collaboration, which can be reinforced by an agile organizational model and will ultimately aid your efforts to build an ecosystem-oriented business.

So, to recap, the changes you need to make concerning talent fall into three main buckets: diversity, openness to new ideas, and predisposition to collaboration. With each of these three areas, the aim is to seek out the kind of people who actively hunger for new challenges, new kinds of experiences, new forms of knowledge, and new connections. In other words, people who will be naturally inclined toward experimentation, who will find new solutions, who will craft innovative new value propositions—and who will thrive in a multifaceted world of ecosystems. And once you've found and hired these people, it is crucial to methodically develop that talent, nurturing employee's strengths and giving them the support they need to adjust for any missteps. As we will see later in this chapter, such an attitude embodies the true spirit of servant leadership—the practice of building people up with support and encouragement rather than motivating them with a punitive, high-pressure environment.

As we've discussed in previous chapters, a world of sectors without borders means that competition may come from unexpected sources—not just from traditional rivals within your industry, but from players in any industry. For that reason, it is vital to have talent who can think multi-dimensionally, who can hold several different frames of reference in their heads at once, and who can execute ambitious, outside-of-the-box ideas. These are the sorts of people who are going to have the creativity to devise inspired solutions in the face of daunting challenges. When it comes to talent, you should not be afraid to think boldly, and to try new, outside-of-the-box ideas.

PERFORMANCE MANAGEMENT

If you have an effective organizational model and the right talent to lead and run it, what else do you need? The next dimension you will need to reconsider as you transform your organization for the ecosystem economy is your performance management process. This can be one of the most difficult adjustments to make, especially for incumbents and those who come from non-startup backgrounds, who are stepping into the ecosystem world after decades of being immersed in the old world of sectors. What looks like failure in the traditional business world may in fact be an indicator of success in the world of ecosystems. Being able to tell the difference and to course-correct, therefore, will be a crucial element of getting ahead. We can divide this proficiency of performance management into four main areas, all of which will need to be examined and retooled in order to be successful in the ecosystem economy. These four areas can be framed as questions: What is your performance management operating cadence? Who is involved? What is covered? And what is your process for following up and consequence management—including incentive alignment to promote and motivate successes and failures?

First, your operating cadence. The ecosystem economy requires that you change every aspect of the way you think about your performance management—and the first and most basic component of that is the frequency with which you conduct performance management sessions. In traditional performance management models, working teams present to leadership in performative, high-stakes monthly or quarterly reviews. By keeping these reviews on such an infrequent cadence, both sides can lose sight of what the real purpose of the review is: to support and sustain the work, and to ensure that everyone is moving together toward the desired results. Such an approach is ill-suited to the ecosystem economy. When you have agile tribes, chapters, and squads working on dynamic, cross-sectoral value propositions, you need to push your performance management process toward a much more frequent operating cadence. As you check in with your teams more and more frequently, those reviews will naturally become more efficient and iterative—more about taking the pulse of your team and finding out what's needed rather than incentivizing them to put on a dog-and-pony show. In the agile model, and especially in the context of the servant leadership mindset, it is not uncommon to have weekly or even more frequent check-ins—not in a punitive or adversarial way, but simply to find whatever roadblocks are standing in the team's way and to ensure that everyone has what they need to move forward.

Next, you need to think about what gets covered in these performance management sessions. What measures are you using to chart your progress? And how does the discussion around them unfold? In traditional performance management models, the measures are frequently more comprehensive than they need to be and mired in bureaucracy. In an ecosystem context, however, you need to focus only on the objectives and key results (OKRs) that are at the core of each agile chapter, tribe, or squad's work. As you do so, remember to always ask yourself: What objective did we give the teams, and what key results are we expecting them to drive?

In addition to pulling leaders' attention away from what matters, focusing on an overly-comprehensive set of measures (or just the wrong ones) can actively hurt your ability to effectively build ecosystem-oriented businesses. There are two common ways this can happen. One is that business leaders will try to measure the success of their ecosystem businesses the same way that they have traditionally measured the success of their core business. They might, for example, demand that any new ecosystem play should immediately have margins comparable to the company' core business. On the other hand, business leaders can convince themselves that they only need to pursue very soft targets: metrics like access, reach, and eyeballs—and in so doing, they can spend lots of time and money on something that never actually creates value. In other words, by using the wrong OKRs (or metrics), companies can convince themselves either that building an ecosystem business is financially impossible, and that there's no point trying—or that doing so will be easy, thereby embarking on a wild goose chase. Instead of falling into either of these traps, ecosystem players need to find a middle road. To do this, you need to understand that there are different stages of building an ecosystem business, and different OKRs that are appropriate for each stage.

At the very beginning, the only OKR that really matters is your effectiveness in delivering basic services and in reaching customers. The goal, at this stage, is simply to become operational. Next, as your ecosystem becomes more established, you will move on to more concrete metrics. You may be giving your ecosystem services away for free at this stage, but perhaps you will begin to see those services steer new customers to your preexisting core business offerings, and bolstering your bottom line there. As you continue on, you will want to start seeing even more concrete results and should therefore starting using some harder metrics. At this stage, you will want to start looking at whether your ecosystem services are generating revenue, and whether they are starting to scale up. Finally, you will start to consider whether your ecosystem is delivering profits. However, throughout all of this, the single most important OKR is the degree to which the ecosystem is creating value. While it is important to use an ever-evolving set of metrics, it is also important not to lose sight of certain fundamental questions: Are we growing the ecosystem? And are we serving the best interests of all key constituents—our partners, our customers, our employees, and the community at large?

But most importantly, at every stage, you need to carefully consider how much value the ecosystem is creating. Measuring that value can be a complicated process, but only by doing so will you be able to truly assess your progress. To do so, you need to consider not only your own revenues and margins, but also the revenues and margins of your partners. You need to consider not only the experience and convenience that you are offering your customers, but also the experience and convenience that your partners are offering. By combining all of that together, you can begin to see the big picture of the value that your ecosystem is creating. After all, the whole rationale behind creating an ecosystem in the first place was the promise of creating more value together than any individual participant is capable of creating on their own.

After considering *what* gets covered, you will need to turn your attention to *who* is involved in the performance management cycle. Traditional performance management models are typically formal and hierarchical—and often involve only the senior management or leadership team. When you're setting up performance management for the ecosystem economy, you need a less hierarchical, more project-oriented, more results-oriented model. You need to involve not just senior management, but also people from all levels within your agile model (e.g., tribes, chapters, and squads). Involving more of the team not only creates a more streamlined and efficient process, but also facilitates an unfiltered flow of information. Management gets an opportunity to hear an unfiltered report straight from the team members who will be best equipped to give it. And the team members get an opportunity to receive feedback and instruction straight from management, without anything getting lost in translation as the information passed through two or three levels of hierarchy and bureaucracy. Obviously there is a limit to how extensively you will be able to do this. If you are a top leader in a fairly large organization that uses the agile model, you may not have the capacity to do this at a squad level, but you might instead choose to do it at a tribe level or for select tribes.

Finally, you will need to adjust your process for following up with your teams. To foster the sort of open, collaborative, ecosystem-friendly environment you need, you have to move away from the sort of evaluatory, punitive relationship that can sometimes arise from the worst sort of traditional performance management process. Instead, you will want to establish a supportive, growth-oriented stance. This is not about sending a message to your teams that they need to meet certain benchmarks, or else. Rather, it's about fostering learning. It's about finding something productive to take away even from a challenging experience. Even when a team fails or falls short of expectations, how can you use that to foster learning and improve the operating model going forward? How are your tribes, chapters, and squads incorporating and building upon those learnings? As we will explore in a later section, these habits will be reinforced when you are able to successfully incorporate a servant leadership mindset into the underlying culture of your organization, but they are worth cultivating on their own. When you follow up with your teams, the goal should be to find answers to these questions: Where are we making progress? Where do we have hurdles? Where could management help—in the true spirit of servant leadership? Lastly, and most importantly, how are you aligning incentives (both tangible and intangible) with overall OKRs and a clear line of sight to keep teams motivated and inspired? Examples of incentives include monetary rewards, recognitions, and career progressions. Much has been written about other incentives, so we won't go into great detail here, but it will suffice to say that you need to strike a fine balance between individual incentives and team incentives.

UNDERLYING CULTURE

Next, you will need to rethink how you are cultivating an underlying culture to sustain the changes you are making within your business. The culture, after all, is what keeps your business going—it is what enables you to perpetuate and build upon all of the other ecosystem opportunities we have discussed. All of the changes and improvements we have discussed up to this point will prove considerably less effective if there is not a strong culture in place to encourage everyone at every level to stay focused on building, refining, and sustaining the ecosystem business. When we say you need to create a culture, what we mean is a shared set of values that drives your work as an organization. According to the *Harvard Business Review*, "culture is an organization's DNA. It is the shared values, goals, attitudes, and practices that characterize a workplace. It is reflected in how people behave, interact with each other, make decisions, and do their work."[8]

At a fundamental level, you need to foster a culture and a set of core values that allow you to take advantage of the ecosystem economy. Some of these core values include: intellectual curiosity, failing fast, servant leadership, teamwork, and long-term thinking. (Of course, some of these overlap with one another, but each is worth considering on its own.) You may wonder: How do these values relate specifically to ecosystems? These can seem almost like universally applicable values. And indeed, on some level, these values all represent good ideas that companies should be pursuing anyway. Even in the past, regardless of ecosystems, implementing a culture based on these values would have had a positive impact on just about any company. But each of these values is critical to laying the foundation for building a successful ecosystem business. In the following, we will go into more detail and explain some but not all of these.

Take intellectual curiosity. We began to cover this a bit in the earlier section on talent. Companies populated by people who are inquisitive and genuinely interested in learning what they can about the world around them are companies that will benefit from the unexpected insights that such curiosity can bring. But if this attitude of curiosity and openness becomes deeply engrained in a company's ethos, it can do even more. When there is a culture of intellectual curiosity and openness in a company employees begin to feel empowered to contribute, to share their ideas, to think outside the box—and ultimately, they will do much more to help grow the pie for everyone.

To be clear: this doesn't mean you should strive for a culture in which employees compete to see who has amassed the most knowledge. Microsoft CEO Satya Nadella has famously declared his intention to cultivate a "learn-it-all" culture rather than a "know-it-all" culture. In an interview with *Business Insider*, he explained that the idea was inspired by the classic book, *Mindset: The New Psychology of Success*, by Stanford professor Carol Dweck. As Nadella recounts, Dweck "describes the simple metaphor of kids at school. One of them is a 'know-it-all' and other is a 'learn-it-all,' and the 'learn-it-all' always will do better than the other one even if the 'know-it-all' kid starts with much more innate capability." Continuing on, he explains how the idea colored his understanding of Microsoft's culture: "If that applies to boys and girls at school, I think it also applies to CEOs, like me, and entire organizations, like Microsoft. We want to be not a 'know-it-all' but 'learn-it-all' organization."[9]

Having a culture that encourages learning for its own sake will naturally lead to new, unexpected, and—in many cases—fruitful opportunities. It is only by building a culture of intellectual curiosity—a learn-it-all culture—that you can find and identify the opportunities you didn't even know about, which may be harboring the greatest rewards of all.

Another value that is key to building an effective culture around ecosystems is the servant leadership mindset. This means taking a holistic view of your employees, learning what they need in order to do their jobs effectively, and figuring out everything you can do to help them reach their full potential. In contrast to the traditional model of leadership, in which the leader's main focus is giving direction and enforcing standards, servant leadership seeks to build employees up—to give them the resources they need to feel comfortable executing the tasks they need to. As the Society for Human Resource Management puts it, leaders who embody this philosophy "possess a serve-first mindset, and they are focused on empowering and uplifting those who work for them. They are serving instead of commanding, showing humility instead of brandishing authority, and always looking to enhance the development of their staff members in ways that unlock potential, creativity and sense of purpose."[10]

The concept of servant leadership was first developed by Robert K. Greenleaf, an AT&T executive who, after retiring in 1964, continued his exploration of what makes leaders and organizations effective. In 1970, he wrote an influential article entitled "The Servant As Leader," in which he laid out his vision of how leaders could change their organizations by dramatically shifting their mindset. In the essay, he observed that attitudes around power and leadership were changing: "A fresh critical look is being taken at the issues of power and authority," he wrote, "and people are beginning to learn, however haltingly, to relate to one another in less coercive and more creatively supporting ways." People working within an organization, he continued, "will freely respond only to individuals who are chosen as leaders because they are proven and trusted as servants. To the extent that this principle prevails in the future, the only truly viable institutions will be those that are predominantly servant-led."[11] According to the nonprofit organization Greenleaf founded, "the key tools for a servant-leader [include] listening, persuasion, access to intuition and foresight, use of language, and pragmatic measurements of outcomes."[12]

In the years since Greenleaf initially proposed the idea, servant leadership has become a hugely influential concept, and has been adopted by businesses and other organizations throughout the world. This however, is more than just a simple tool to motivate employees to work hard; rather, it is part of a comprehensive leadership strategy of lifting employees up and giving them the tools they need to be successful in their roles. And beyond boosting performance and improving morale, it can help foster the next generation of leaders by creating a supportive, open environment in which employees can climb into positions of greater responsibility as they learn and grow over the years.

Adopting the principles of servant leadership can help your organization to meet the demands of the new ecosystem economy in much the same way that encouraging intellectual curiosity can. Ecosystems require organizations that are constantly on the lookout for new possibilities, constantly scanning the horizon for new opportunities to make cross-sectoral plays and forge cooperative partnerships with others. Organizations can only be open to those possibilities and opportunities when their employees are curious and open minded. And employees are most likely to be curious and open minded when their leaders are holistically looking out for their best interests and actively searching for ways to provide them with everything they need. This is clearly most relevant to those within the senior ranks of your organization, but it really applies to everyone who serves in key roles. Above all, servant leadership helps organizations adopt all of the ideals that the ecosystem economy demands: openness, entrepreneurialism, decisiveness, a fail-fast mindset, long-term thinking, and more.

One of the other important values to adopt within your organization's culture is a fail-fast mentality. The concept of failing fast has its origins in the Silicon Valley world of startups, where upstart entrepreneurs developed an ethos of embracing failure as a means of getting closer and closer to a truly brilliant ideas through an iterative series of attempts, failures, and readjustments. The concept is often encapsulated in the mantra, "fail fast, fail often." The key, however, is in the "fast" part—you need to proceed through the "failure" part as quickly, efficiently, and painlessly as possible. As *Forbes* contributor Dan Pontefract notes, the concept is frequently misunderstood. "The real aim of 'fail fast, fail often,' is not to fail, but to be iterative," he writes. "To succeed, we must be open to failure—sure—but the intention is to ensure we are learning from our mistakes as we tweak, reset, and then redo if necessary. When executives institute a 'fail fast, fail often' mantra, they must ensure it is not at the expense of creative or critical thinking."[13]

When done right, enshrining a fail-fast mentality as part of your organization's culture will actually boost those powers of creative and critical thinking—and this is precisely why doing so is essential to succeeding in the ecosystem economy. To leverage the exciting new possibilities and opportunities that ecosystems bring, you need employees who have the freedom to experiment and the boldness to try new ideas with full knowledge that these experiments may not pan out. And to sustain an ecosystem play over the long haul, you need a culture that fosters that bold, creative, independently-minded spirit on a large scale. You need an organization that instills those values as a matter of habit.

Finally, any successful culture building effort focused on the ecosystem economy needs to promote long-term thinking. Rather than concentrating their energies on meeting narrow targets in the immediate future in order to impress their bosses and advance their own career prospects, employees should be focused on creating something sustainable—something that contributes value for everyone involved. This is particularly important in the context of ecosystems since, as we previously explained, building an ecosystem requires adjusting your expectations in the short term. You may have to sacrifice in the immediate future in order to lay the foundation for a successful ecosystem business later on.

SUPPORTING INFRASTRUCTURE

But even having the proper organizational structure, the right people to work within it, the right performance management model, and the right underlying culture isn't enough. The people within your organization still need to have the right tools. To truly succeed in the ecosystem economy, you need to transform your infrastructure—you have to completely rewire the company for the new reality you are living in.

It is important to distinguish here between ecosystem-oriented infrastructure improvements and the updates and reforms businesses should already be undertaking, simply to contend with the otherwise rapidly shifting business environment. Quite apart from the pressures and incentives of the ecosystem economy, businesses as a general matter need to rethink their IT, tech, and data infrastructure. Many of these imperatives will be familiar, even obvious: businesses need to evolve their IT systems, making them more agile and modular. They need to add the systems and the support structures that are necessary to serve customers and partners alike—and they especially need to make it easier for partner businesses to connect to their value propositions. However, when we consider the transformational changes that the ecosystem economy will bring, we can see that businesses must go even further. The improvements that they need to make in that respect fall into two main groups: internally-oriented and externally-oriented infrastructure.

Let us begin with externally-oriented infrastructure. In the ecosystem economy, connectivity is paramount. Because ecosystems are networks of interdependent businesses working together to create value, the exact means by which those businesses are connected matter a great deal. To give your customers as many options as possible, and the strongest, most comprehensive value proposition you can, your goal should be to make it as easy as possible for other players to connect in. This is, essentially, a matter of supporting and enabling your partners. You want other businesses, as much as possible, to be able to participate in your ecosystem on a "plug and play" basis.

Another critical element of evolving your externally-oriented infrastructure is building into it effective practices around handling data. Again, quite apart from the concerns and pressures of the ecosystem economy, all businesses need to pay more attention to data—how they collect it, how they maintain and clean it, how they analyze it, and how they integrate it into their different business processes. But if you are an ecosystem player, all of this becomes exponentially more difficult, more complex, and more important. The goal of an ecosystem play is to own the customer—to convince customers and partners to use your ecosystem for all needs at every step of their journey. To own the customer, you need to know the customer. And to know the customer, you need data. Data is the number one weapon in the fight to own customers. To effectively wield this weapon, though, you need not only to collect, maintain, and analyze the data; you need a strong, externally-facing infrastructure capable of controlling how these data flow through your ecosystem. And you need an infrastructure that effectively manages how the different participants in your ecosystem are able to share and collaboratively use those data. The danger you need to avoid at all costs is letting data get siloed, or trapped within one part of the ecosystem, when it could be put to work more productively elsewhere. If you are running an ecosystem with many different parts and many different services, you need infrastructure to connect them—you need to ensure that incentives are properly aligned so that data are able to flow freely between those different parts as needed.

But you also need to evolve your internally-oriented infrastructure. This can include functions like finance, accounting, legal, and more. Consider financial infrastructure, for instance. If you are an incumbent making an ecosystem play, you probably have both a core, traditional business and a separate unit focused on building an ecosystem business. To succeed with your ecosystem play, you will need to find ways of ensuring that each unit has an appropriate means of measuring its financial progress.

Or take the question of legal matters. Ecosystems involve huge legal complexities, and if they are not handled correctly, these could create an overwhelming burden. Imagine, for example, that you are a company preparing to make an ecosystem play. You probably already have some partners, and a legal framework to manage those relationships, for which you employ a team of lawyers to help maintain. However, in order to make your ecosystem play, you will need to drastically boost the number of partnerships you are engaged in—perhaps by ten times or more what you have now. If you are prudent and forward-thinking, chances are you will be prepared for this. But, at the same time, you will need to consider: do you really want to involve ten times as many lawyers to manage those new partnerships? Almost certainly not. For that reason, you will need to radically rethink the scalability of your legal process. So it will be with other processes, too. As the emerging ecosystem economy continues to transform how business is done on a daily basis, you will need to rethink the infrastructure needed to support your organizational model, the underlying culture you are trying to build, and your approach to talent. Doing so will help you to deal with ever-increasing levels of complexity and the constantly-shifting landscape. This will mean adopting new infrastructure practices such as taking advantage of new and evolving digital tools for managing processes like finance, legal, HR, and more.

Once you have reinvented your approach to your organizational and operating model, talent, performance management, culture, and supporting infrastructure, you will have taken the first steps toward reinventing your business for the ecosystem economy. But these are still only the first steps. As we've suggested in previous chapters as well, you should think of this, too, as an iterative, ongoing process. You may need to cycle through reflecting on each of these categories several times before you can be sure that you've identified the best path forward. However, you have by this this point considered all of the major questions that may arise when thinking about how to navigate the new environment and build a successful ecosystem business. We've taken you through choosing where to play, evolving your proposition, determining your role, picking partners, and thinking through how to transform your organization. In other words, we've taken you through the "where," the "with whom," and the "how." Now all that's left is the execution. It's time to go out there and build a successful ecosystem business! Let's get to work—there's no time to waste.

THINGS TO WATCH OUT FOR WHEN TRANSFORMING THE ORGANIZATION

1. **Being too focused on the short-term:** As we've said before, building a successful ecosystem business requires perseverance and long-term thinking. It requires looking ahead, and seeing that the new propositions you are building cannot immediately be judged by the same standards used to evaluate your current business. Therefore, you must lay out the potential growth trajectory of your ecosystem carefully with reasonable milestones that are appropriate for long-term potential and derive OKRs from them. This is not to say that long-term thinking should drive your decisions entirely, but you do need to strike a tight balance between long-term and short-term parameters in order to judge your progress effectively. It is only by doing this that you will be able to make the right calls and lead your business in the right direction.

2. **Outsourcing the work of building an ecosystem to technology suppliers:** Some companies recognize the importance of ecosystems but lack the resolve to prepare—and therefore look for quick and easy solutions, ways of appearing as though they are taking the issue seriously. One of the most common of these superficial solutions is to hand off the real work of building an ecosystem business to technology partners. As we covered in Chapters 4 and 5, many companies will need to bring in an ecosystem partner to supply the critical backbone or platform for a new ecosystem proposition. But it is easy to succumb to the temptation of letting that partner or supplier drive the ecosystem building—or at least absolve you of the responsibility of doing so.

3. **Not having a means to measure holistic impact:** Many companies recognize the vital importance of measuring their performance, and yet fail to develop the proper comprehensive metrics for assessing how both they and their partners are doing in terms of value creation. Oftentimes we see companies only giving lip service to the idea of

effective performance management, without truly internalizing how it should be leveraged to maximize value for all key constituents (e.g., customers, partners, other stakeholders).

4. **Building ecosystem businesses too far or too close:** As we have already alluded to, one of the most prevalent mistakes that organizations make is choosing the wrong place for their ecosystem builds. This tends to have a devastating effect, setting these efforts up to fail before they even get off the ground. Building too close to the core business line causes problems as managers trying to juggle new initiatives on the side struggle with prioritization, while the traditional nature of the core organization makes attracting ecosystem-oriented talent a challenge. At the same time, building too far from the organization also leads to failure, making it impossible to leverage synergies or connect new ideas back to the core business, while also causing problems with data sharing and internal transfer taxation. Overall, it can be extremely difficult to align incentives and support collaboration when the businesses are culturally and operationally too far from each other.

5. **Failing slow:** Most traditional businesses have a culture of not accepting failure, which sometimes leads them to declare new business projects successful even when they plainly are not. This incentivizes company leaders to do all sorts of irrational things, like inefficiently allocating resources, investing imprudently in struggling ecosystem businesses, and—perhaps most importantly—pulling resources and management attention away from promising new ventures by keeping them focused on old, failing ones that everyone is too proud to admit are failing. Only radical transparency and not just the acceptance but celebration of failures can help here.

Ten Time-Tested Principles for the Emerging Ecosystem Economy

Finding Prosperity in a World of Sectors Without Borders

We hope that by now you have a sense, not only of the transformative power of ecosystems, but also of the path that you might take toward building your own successful ecosystem business.

Over the course of this book, we've frequently emphasized both the exciting opportunities and the potential threats that the ecosystem economy presents. Ecosystems, we'll recall, are communities of interconnected digital and physical business that work across the boundaries between traditional sectors of the economy to meet customer needs holistically. It's true that if you fail to take seriously the monumental shift they represent, you could place your business in great peril. And it's also true that if you carefully track new developments in the economy, and play your cards right, ecosystems could bring you great success and prosperity.

As we mentioned at the outset, there is potentially $70–100 trillion in gross economic output (as measured in revenue) at stake over the next few decades. The potential of the ecosystem economy means not only increased competition, but also more freedom to devise new and creative value propositions that leverage emerging technologies to solve previously insurmountable problems—or meet latent, not fully realized customer needs. Finding your way in this new economy means not only a huge opportunity to grow your business, but also an important chance to serve society and contribute to the greater good.

This book, you will recall, is divided into two parts. In Part One, we laid out for you the grand narrative of how ecosystems emerged, how they are transforming the economy, and how they will continue to transform it in the future.

First, we went all the way back to the early days of human civilization to get a sense of just how enduring of a feature economic sectors have been over the millennia. Just about everything else has changed about the way we, as humans, live—but sectors remained discrete, separate entities. Some may have changed, while others disappeared or arose with various technological developments, but across all those many years, sectors were, for the most part, clearly demarcated—it was always easy to tell where one ended and another began. That is, until very recently. In the early twenty-first century, something changed: technological advancements and changing customer expectations allowed businesses to break through the walls that had previously been keeping sectors separate. Companies could finally work across sectors to meet customer needs on a deeper and more fundamental level—that is to say, they began to group customer needs into sets that logically fit together, and devised ways of serving those needs all together, as part of a single, integrated proposition. Previously, sectors had been a remarkably consistent fact of life in human society, but there were some entities that managed to transcend their boundaries. There were, for example, conglomerates—or firms composed of multiple different, but unrelated, lines of business. But unlike ecosystems, their different parts in many cases did not fit together naturally, and their core purpose was not driven by meeting end-to-end holistic customer needs.

After exploring this backstory and its significance, we looked at the recent explosion of ecosystems and how they're reshaping the world around us. It was not until the late 2000s, with the rise of smartphones and other important technological developments, that the true potential of ecosystems began to be unleashed. As the first ecosystem companies began to form, they brought to the world an unprecedented level of convenience: for the first time, we began to see breakthroughs like smartphones, app stores, and mobile-based ridesharing and food-delivery services. As consumers came to expect this level of convenience, that expectation drove a demand for even more powerful technologies. Before long, the consumer demand for more convenience and the acceleration of technological progress were building off of each other, creating a positive upward spiral of ecosystem growth.

Today we are beginning to see the incredible results of this virtuous cycle—but what we see now is only a brief glimmer of what ecosystems will achieve in the future. As technological progress continues to accelerate, and as consumers become ever more expectant of the conveniences that cross-sectoral propositions bring, we have every reason to expect that ecosystems will become an even more dominant feature of our economic life. As this begins to play out, and as the borders between sectors continue to dissolve, we can see that the economy is reorganizing itself around dynamic new configurations centered on fundamental human needs. With the help of psychology's insights about these needs, we can anticipate what some of these new ecosystems that are forming will be. We expect approximately twelve major ecosystems. What exactly these ecosystems look like will depend on a host of uncertainties: the geopolitical outcomes of the next few decades, including whether the world becomes more globalized or more regionalized; the trajectory of income inequality and its repercussions; how governments around the world change their approach to regulation, especially around data; how successfully humanity is able to muster an effective response to the problem of climate change; and how quickly and effectively we are able to leverage advances in artificial intelligence, biotechnology, and nanotechnology. Developments in each of these areas will have a significant effect on the future of ecosystems—and a breakthrough could catalyze a new ecosystem revolution.

After exploring the past, present, and future of ecosystems, we moved into Part Two of the book, where we took you through the real-world implications of the ecosystem revolution and gave you a guidebook for how to navigate it. The first step in that process consists of choosing where to play and identifying what you will do to evolve your value proposition. As you think through this, you must start with the basics: take a step back and consider how your customer base is changing—and how your customers' needs are changing—given the ongoing technology trends. Then ask yourself where you have opportunities to offer compelling and differentiated customer propositions—irrespective of existing sector borders. Once you have identified some promising possibilities, prioritize them based on any advantages you might have and where you see opportunities for such a proposition to thrive. Next, you need to decide: For you to offer that differentiated proposition, do you need an ecosystem or not? And if you do need an ecosystem, can you use an existing ecosystem, or do you need to build one? With that determination made, you need to size up the competition and determine where you have the best possible opportunity to make a difference for your customers. To arrive at a compelling and differentiated proposition, you may need to cycle through these steps a few times, ensuring that you are considering every possible angle.

With your new value proposition identified, and the question of whether or not you need an ecosystem answered, you have your objective. Now you need to get there. The next step is to determine what role you are best suited to playing in the new ecosystem you are envisioning. Do you aspire to orchestrate an ecosystem, with all of the opportunities and responsibility that role entails? Or are you content to be a participant in someone else's ecosystem and accept whatever drawbacks such a position brings with it? Or do you belong somewhere in between? Your first task in making this determination is identifying the assets and capabilities needed for the ecosystem to function. For each, consider what the best way of obtaining it would be: developing it yourself, acquiring another business that already has it, or forming an ecosystem partnership. If some of the most critical assets and capabilities are ones that will need to be obtained through ecosystem partnerships, that may be a sign that orchestration would be challenging from your current position.

Finally, you must transform your organization from the inside out, shifting your focus from the old world of sectors to the new world of ecosystems. This begins with the way your business structure is organized. You need to cut out the clunky, old-fashioned bureaucratic systems and instead use an agile approach—forming dynamic, fast-moving, and self-organizing teams that work collaboratively and non-hierarchically (as we explained, these are organized into tribes, chapters, and squads). You need to reimagine your approach to talent, seeking out employees with a diversity of experience, thought, and background; the curiosity to learn more; and a deep desire to collaborate across borders—whether interdepartmental or between sectors of the economy. In short, you need talent who are open to seeing new possibilities and ready to form unexpected and unorthodox connections in the service of delivering greater value. And you need leaders who are committed to providing their team members with unwavering constructive support—in the true spirit of servant leadership. Next, changing your organization for the ecosystem economy also means changing your performance management—and finding new and more effective ways of tracking your progress. Instead of overly-complicated, performative review sessions, you need a streamlined, practical, and iterative process centered on giving leaders a clear sense of where they can be helpful and where they should get out of the way. With all of this done, you need to lay the foundation to ensure that the process of change and adjustment remains ongoing. You need to foster a culture to sustain the transformation, promoting values of intellectual curiosity, failing fast, servant leadership, and long-term thinking. And finally, you next need to rewire your company's supporting infrastructure, developing entirely new internally-oriented and externally-oriented systems to help you adapt to the new world of ecosystems.

Again, this is intended to be an iterative, ongoing process. We will not pretend that after going through it once you will immediately identify the perfect path forward. But by cycling through the steps multiple times, thinking through your situation from several different angles, and considering all the different potential scenarios, you will soon arrive at some well-reasoned, nuanced insights that will give you the best possible shot at success.

Such a drastic reevaluation is made necessary by enormous shifts happening in the economy today. Again, as we noted earlier in the book, if you look at the top ten companies worldwide today in terms of market cap, you are likely to find that a significant majority of them are ecosystem businesses. This stands in stark contrast to how the same list looked a decade or two ago, when it was dominated by non-ecosystem players like oil and gas companies. And the explosive growth of ecosystems will only continue, generating a multitude of possibilities for meeting latent customer needs and contributing to the good of society. Key aspects of the economy are changing, and there is an enormous amount of value at stake. Again, over the next few decades, we expect that the global revenue pool of the integrated network economy will reach $70–100 trillion. Whether you are interested in getting a piece of that, or simply hoping to solve big societal problems like climate change, the following principles should be of great interest.

TEN TIME-TESTED PRINCIPLES FOR THE ECOSYSTEM ECONOMY

To distill the lessons of our ecosystem playbook down even more, we can boil its processes and recommendations down to a set of ten key principles. We believe the following principles capture the essence of the insights and methods we have described throughout the book. We hope that over the course of reading the book, you will have already gained a full appreciation of why these principles matter and how exactly they help. But it can also be helpful to look back on what you've learned for a quick sense of the most important steps you need to take and the processes you need to adopt.

One: Start with the customer and end with the customer

In the ecosystem economy, customers and their needs should be the highest of all priorities. Ecosystem businesses should be designed around the value propositions you are making to your customers. They should be a means to enhance your offering and not something to pursue just because other businesses are. Don't solve your business problem; solve the customer's problem. Every move you make when building an ecosystem should be directed toward making life easier and more convenient for your customers—which in turn makes your offer more compelling and differentiated.

Two: Choose your role wisely

That is, be realistic. In Chapter 5, we went into detail on how to decide where you belong on the spectrum between ecosystem orchestrator and ecosystem participant. The reality is that many companies simply cannot be ecosystem orchestrators. By definition, only a small handful of businesses will be ideally positioned to orchestrate *and* have the assets, resources, and capabilities needed to do so. We all want to be in charge—but if every company tried to orchestrate, they all would fail. And if you're not set up to orchestrate, expending a great deal of time and money trying to do so will be a colossal waste of resources. Better to devote your energies where they will be most productive. For help in making this determination carefully and deliberately, you can consult the process and criteria that we laid out in Chapter 5.

Three: Think and act in platforms both physical and digital

If you want to be successful in the new ecosystem economy, then developing, fostering, and enhancing platforms will give you the necessary foundation to do so. Platforms come in various shapes and forms. As we discussed earlier, having a platform or backbone helps put you in position to be an orchestrator, and significantly boosts your chances of being able to control your own destiny and shape the value-creation equation. As you evolve your business, choosing where and how to make investments, you must think in terms of how you are positioning yourself to deliver value for your platform participants and your customers.

Four: Go all in—set up right and make ecosystems a top priority for you and your leadership team

If you've decided that you need an ecosystem in order to adapt to the new economy, then setting up such a play and making it successful should be at the top of the agenda for the CEO and the board. Don't delegate this task or push it down to be a concern only for the lower levels of your organization. But also make sure you have enough business-building capacity with the freedom to operate outside of the traditional, core business's domain. This can be a tricky balancing act. To successfully strike the right balance, you will need to embody a true entrepreneurial spirit and wholeheartedly embrace the fail-fast mentality. Most companies struggle to effectively divide their focus between transforming and continuing on with their core businesses. But you have to do both. And most importantly, you have to go all-in on ecosystems.

Five: Identify and leverage control points

While building your ecosystem business, you need to pay close attention to the control points—like data. That is to say, identify the key steps in the customer journey that, if you control them, will allow you to gain an advantage over your competitors and form a deeper, closer relationship with your customers by meeting their needs holistically. Typically, important data sets make good control points. Therefore, you must identify and pursue the especially important data sets that will offer deeper and more meaningful insights into your customers' needs. And beyond data sets, there could be many other things (e.g., access to customers) that could function as control points.

Six: Don't confuse vendor-customer relationships with ecosystems

The constraints and hassles of managing a company on a day-to-day basis often push business leaders to be short-sighted. It is easy, therefore, to ignore the warning signs and fool yourself into believing that you are already doing enough to adapt to the ecosystem economy. You must therefore avoid fooling yourself into thinking that your vendor-customer relationships are ecosystem partnerships. If you typically are dealing with your partners within an RFP-based approach, more than likely, they are not true ecosystem partners—at least not according to the way we define the term. Typically, ecosystem partners should be defined by deep collaboration at a fundamental level, as we described in earlier chapters. Hold the bar high—and do everything you can to rise to the challenge.

Seven: Be clear-eyed about where you need vertical integration and where you need ecosystems

Both can co-exist peacefully, but they are not the same. As we covered in Chapter 5, when you don't have the necessary capabilities to build your ecosystem business, you have three options: you can obtain them by forming an ecosystem partnership, develop them on your own, or acquire another business that already has them. In some cases, it may be easier or more cost effective to develop the capabilities yourself (i.e., vertically integrate), while in others, it may be best to acquire them from outside or form ecosystem partnerships. Apple, for instance, has done both—opting to design its own chips for its devices, but choosing to rely on ecosystem relationships for the apps in its App Store. Think carefully and choose wisely which approach is needed whenever you are faced with the need to obtain new capabilities.

Eight: Constantly reevaluate your position

In the world of ecosystems, you need to be continually reassessing your role and your position. In this new world, the speed at which your opportunities are shifting and reconfiguring is much faster than in the old world of sectors. If your value propositions involve multiple sectors, there are that many more startups, regulatory changes, conditions, and complexities to consider. You need to be constantly reevaluating where you are by incorporating the changes around you and refining your approach and focus. As you continue this process, you may find it useful to engage in some more practical, future-oriented exercises, like war-gaming or red team strategy sessions.

Nine: Avoid incrementalism

You can't take baby steps. In every aspect of how you approach your ecosystem business, you need to be ready to make big, ambitious moves. First, aim high in terms of the value proposition you are looking to deliver. Second, be ambitious in terms of the partnerships you pursue and how you structure those relationships. And, third, be ambitious in terms of developing, fostering, growing, and maintaining the ecosystem. Of course, this will require resources, time, and commitment—and if you are unwilling to put in the work and make that investment, you will risk falling into the trap of incrementalism. Many business leaders will try to execute ecosystem plays in a very incremental manner—by, for example, trying to establish only a handful of ecosystem partnerships without truly committing the necessary resources to the task of building an ecosystem business. Such a half-hearted effort—especially on the part of a prospective orchestrator—will almost certainly fail to produce meaningful results. And it will hold you back in innumerable other ways, too—for instance, making it extremely difficult for you to attract and retain talent.

Ten: Put value creation over profits

For you to be successful, you need to let value creation guide you at every step along the way. By this we mean value creation not only for customers but also for all ecosystem partners. Value creation comes in many forms—for instance, making it easier for your partners to work with you is a form of value creation. As is making it easier for your partners to offer propositions to your customers.

Once you've thought through the implications of each of these principles, it's time to begin the challenging task of applying them to yourself. How can you use each of these ten principles in your own work? How can you apply them in your ordinary, day-to-day activities? To begin to understand how, you might turn each principle into a question and direct it back on yourself:

1. How are you starting and ending with the customers? Especially in terms of focusing on the right segments and driving great experience and engagement in the true spirit of delivering unprecedented value?

2. How certain are you that you're choosing a role that is appropriate for you? How can you make sure you're being neither overly ambitious nor overly cautious in selecting your role?

3. How well are you developing, fostering, and investing in the platform in the true interest of promoting the ecosystem and creating value for all key constituents? (This is, of course, especially important if you aspire to be an orchestrator.)

4. Are you, as an organization, giving the right priority for ecosystem business development? In reality, what portion of your time is truly spent focused on building and growing the ecosystem?

5. What are the control points, and why are they important in enhancing customer value propositions and your competitive propositions? And how well positioned are you to leverage these control points?

6. How are your vendor relationships different from your ecosystem relationships? If they're not meaningfully different, your "ecosystem partnerships" are probably not really ecosystem partnerships—and you will need to adjust course to make sure you develop deeper relationships.

7. Where are you using an ecosystem approach, and where are you using vertical integration—in the true interest of delivering value for your customers and partners? And why?

8. How often are you evaluating your efforts to build an ecosystem business? If it is every two to three years, that is likely too infrequent. If it is every month, that is likely too often. How can you strike the right balance?

9. How ambitious are you in your efforts to develop your ecosystem business? Do your ambitions scare you? If not, chances are you approach is too cautious, too incremental.

10. How well are you doing in putting value creation (for both customers and partners) ahead of profits?

And with these time-tested principles, you should now have the direction and purpose you need to find success in the ecosystem economy. As we have demonstrated throughout this book, we are living through a singular historical moment. Enormous economic forces that have been shaping human experience for hundreds of years are starting to shift. Just by taking the time to read this book, you have already taken the first step on your journey toward understanding these shifts, and finding a way through them. The path ahead will be difficult, but it is also full of excitement and possibility.

There is tremendous potential waiting out there for you to discover. Your task now is to go out, find it, and put to good use—both for the benefit of your customers and for the benefit of society as a whole. By leveraging the emerging ecosystem economy you will be able to maximize your efforts to change the world for the better. Now, let's roll up our sleeves, and get to work.

Acknowledgments

Throughout the process of conceiving, planning, writing, and publishing this book, we have relied on a generous and dedicated group of friends, family, colleagues, and other experts who have lent support, guidance, and inspiration.

In particular, we are grateful to numerous colleagues at McKinsey and Company, which has been our professional home for many years. These include numerous colleagues from the firm's Global Banking practice; from the Tech, Media, and Telecom practice; and from the Corporate Finance and Strategy Practice. Of course, the team within McKinsey that has been most central to the development of this book project has been the Ecosystem Strategy Hub. We extend our sincere thanks to the entire team, but we are especially grateful to its leader and a key content contributor to the book, Istvan Rab, and other thought leaders, Violet Chung, Ulrike Deetjen, Tamas Kabay, and Imre Szilvacsku for their deep insight, sharp observations, and helpful contributions. We are also grateful to our incredible executive assistants, Brianna Rodriguez and Csilla Szaraz, whose capable management and organization helped to make this book a reality.

Once the idea for this project was born, the long process of developing it into a full-fledged book began. We are grateful to several people who played vital roles along the way: to Raju Narisetti, the head of McKinsey Global Publishing, who provided crucial guidance and helped point us to some of the other indispensable team members; to Bill Falloon, our fearless editor at John Wiley & Sons, who provided invaluable support, sharp feedback, and an expert perspective on the business book market; to Samantha Wu and Purvi Patel, also of the Wiley team, whose professionalism and capable management made the publication process as smooth as possible; to independent editor Connor Guy, whose storytelling excellence made this unique story come to life; to the talented copyediting team at Cape Cod Compositors, whose diligence and rigorous scrutiny improved the book immeasurably; and to Jonathon Berlin, who helped create the many beautiful charts and illustrations.

Finally, we could not have finished such a daunting project without the loving support of our families: Vyjayanthi, Anisha, Shalini, Shrihan, Judit, Andor, Emma, and Ádám.

List of Illustrations

Notes

INTRODUCTION

1. Trinidad, K. (2020). History of the Supermarket Industry in America. *Stacker*. (13 March). www.stacker.com/stories/3984/history-supermarket-industry-america (accessed 29 October 2021).
2. Companiesmarketcap.com. (2022). Largest Companies by Market Cap. www.companiesmarketcap.com (accessed 23 February 2022).
3. McKinsey analysis, IHS World Industry Service. (2022).

CHAPTER 1

1. Hobbes, T. (1651). *Leviathan*. Project Gutenberg. www.gutenberg.org/files/3207/3207-h/3207-h.htm (accessed 23 February 2022).
2. Violatti, C. (2018). Neolithic Period. *World History Encyclopedia* (2 April). www.worldhistory.org/Neolithic/ (accessed 15 September 2021).
3. Carozza, P. Roman Law. *Encyclopedia Britannica*. www.britannica.com/topic/collegia (accessed 15 September 2021).
4. *Encyclopedia Britannica*. Personal Computer. www.britannica.com/technology/personal-computer (accessed 15 September 2021).
5. Hadas, E. (2018). Conglomerates Will Never Die. *New York Times* (12 December). www.nytimes.com/2018/12/12/business/dealbook/conglomerates-will-never-die.html (accessed 16 September 2021).
6. Bown, S. (2010). *Merchant Kings: When Companies Ruled the World, 1600–1900*. New York: Thomas Dunne Books. p. 16.

7. Atsushi, O. (2013). The Dutch East India Company and the Rise of Intra-Asian Commerce. *Nippon.com* (18 September). www.nippon.com/en/features/c00105/ (accessed 20 September 2021).

8. Taylor, B. (2013). The Rise and Fall of the Largest Corporation in History. *Business Insider* (6 November). www.businessinsider.com/rise-and-fall-of-united-east-india-2013-11 (accessed 20 September 2021).

9. Davis, G., Diekmann, K., and Tinsley, C. (1994). The Decline and Fall of the Conglomerate Firm in the 1980s: The Deinstitutionalization of an Organizational Form. *American Sociological Review* 59 (4): pp. 547–8. www.jstor.org/stable/2095931 (accessed 20 September 2021).

10. Hurley, T. (2006). The Urge to Merge: Contemporary Theories on the Rise of Conglomerate Mergers in the 1960s. *Journal of Business and Technology Law* 1 (1): p. 186. www.digitalcommons.law.umaryland.edu/cgi/viewcontent.cgi?referer=&httpsredir=1&article=1014&context=jbtl (accessed 21 September 2021).

11. *The Economist*. (1997). Harold Geneen (4 December). https://www.economist.com/obituary/1997/12/04/harold-geneen (accessed 21 September 2021).

12. Cane, J. (2011). ITT, the Ever-Shrinking Conglomerate. *New York Times* (12 January). https://dealbook.nytimes.com/2011/01/12/itt-the-ever-shrinking-conglomerate/ (accessed 21 September 2021).

13. Gabler, N. (2006). *Walt Disney: The Triumph of American Imagination*. New York: Knopf.

14. Titizian, J. (2013). Disneyland, The Quintessential Classics: Mickey Mouse. The Walt Disney Family Museum (3 April). www.waltdisney.org/blog/disneyland-quintessential-classics-mickey-mouse (accessed 22 September 2021).

15. Zenger, T. (2013). The Disney Recipe. *Harvard Business Review* (28 May). www.hbr.org/2013/05/what-makes-a-good-corporate-st (accessed 22 September 2021).

16. Ramachandran, J., Manikandan, K.S., and Pant, A. (2013). Why Conglomerates Thrive (Outside the US). *Harvard Business Review* (December). www.hbr.org/2013/12/why-conglomerates-thrive-outside-the-us (accessed 23 September 2021).

17. Addicott, D. (2017). The Rise and Fall of the Zaibatsu: Japan's Industrial and Economic Modernization. *Global Tides* 11 (5). www.digitalcommons.pepperdine.edu/cgi/viewcontent.cgi?article=1259&context=globaltides (accessed 23 September 2021). Encyclopedia Britannica. Zaibatsu. www.britannica.com/topic/zaibatsu (accessed 24 September 2021).

18. Albert, E. (2018). South Korea's Chaebol Challenge. Council on Foreign Relations (4 May). www.cfr.org/backgrounder/south-koreas-chaebol-challenge (accessed 24 September 2021).

19. Hadas, E. (2018). Conglomerates Will Never Die. *New York Times* (12 December). www.nytimes.com/2018/12/12/business/dealbook/conglo merates-will-never-die.html (accessed 24 September 2021).

20. Halton, C. (2021). Conglomerate Boom. *Investopedia* (15 September). www.investopedia.com/terms/c/conglomerate-boom.asp (accessed 25 September 2021).

21. Ramachandran, Manikandan, and Pant (2013).

22. Behr, P. (1988). Wave of Mergers, Takeovers is a Part of Reagan Legacy. *Washington Post* (30 October). www.washingtonpost.com/archive/business/1988/10/30/wave-of-mergers-takeovers-is-a-part-of-reagan-legacy/e90598c2-628d-40fe-b9c6-a621e298671d/ (accessed 25 September 2021).

23. Davis, Diekmann, and Tinsley (1994).

24. Chen, J. (2021). Conglomerate Discount. *Investopedia* (28 February). www.investopedia.com/terms/c/conglomeratediscount.asp (accessed 25 September 2021).

25. *The Economist*. (1991). A Survey of International Finance: The Ebb Tide (27 April).

26. Ramachandran, Manikandan, and Pant (2013).

27. Ramachandran Manikandan, and Pant (2013).

CHAPTER 2

1. Kahney, L. (2004). Inside Look at Birth of iPod. *Wired* (21 July). www.wired.com/2004/07/inside-look-at-birth-of-the-ipod/ (accessed 13 September 2021).

2. Farber, D. (2014). When iPhone Met World, Seven Years Ago Today. *CNET* (9 January). www.cnet.com/news/when-iphone-met-world-7-years-ago-today/ (accessed 13 September 2021).

3. Woyke, E. (2009). A Brief History of the BlackBerry. *Forbes* (17 August). www.forbes.com/2009/08/17/rim-apple-sweeny-intelligent-technology-blackberry.html?sh=6d621579863e (accessed 14 September 2021).

4. Isaacson, W. (2011). *Steve Jobs: The Exclusive Biography*. New York: Simon & Schuster, p. 501.

5. Bonnington, C. (2013). Five Years On, the App Store Has Forever Changed the Face of Software. *Wired* (10 July). www.wired.com/2013/07/five-years-of-the-app-store/ (accessed 14 September 2021).

6. Fuller, A., Fan, Z., Day, C., and Barlow, C. (2020). Digital Twin: Enabling Technologies, Challenges, and Open Research. *IEEE Access* 8. www.ieeexplore.ieee.org/stamp/stamp.jsp?tp=&arnumber=9103025 (accessed 15 September 2021).

7. O'Neill, A. (2022). World: Total Population from 2010 to 2020. *Statista* (23 February). www.statista.com/statistics/805044/total-population-worldwide/ (accessed 27 February 2022).
   Vailshery, L.S. (2021). Internet of Things (IoT) and Non-IoT Active Device Connections Worldwide from 2010 to 2025. *Statista* (8 March). www.statista.com/statistics/1101442/iot-number-of-connected-devices-worldwide/ (accessed 27 February 2022).

8. Lueth, K.L. (2020). State of the IoT 2020: 12 Billion IoT Connections, Surpassing Non-IoT for the First Time. *IoT Analytics* (19 November). www.iot-analytics.com/state-of-the-iot-2020-12-billion-iot-connections-surpassing-non-iot-for-the-first-time/ (accessed 27 February 2022).

9. Sinha, S. (2021). State of IoT 2021: Number of Connected IoT Devices Growing 9% to 12.3 Billion Globally, Cellular IoT Now Surpassing 2 Billion. *IoT Analytics* (22 September). www.iot-analytics.com/number-connected-iot-devices/ (accessed 27 February 2022).
   United Nations Department of Economic and Social Affairs. (2019). World Population Prospects: 2019. www.un.org/en/desa/world-population-prospects-2019-highlights (accessed 27 February 2022).

10. Press, G. (2021). 54 Predictions about the State of Data in 2021. *Forbes* (30 December). https://www.forbes.com/sites/gilpress/2021/12/30/54-predictions-about-the-state-of-data-in-2021/ (accessed 27 February 2022).

11. Reinhardt, A. (1998). Steve Jobs: There's Sanity Returning. *Businessweek* (25 May). www.bloomberg.com/news/articles/1998-05-25/steve-jobs-theres-sanity-returning (accessed 27 February 2022).

12. Bhargava, S., Finneman, B., Schmidt, J., et al. (2020). The Young and the Restless: Generation Z in America. McKinsey (20 March). www.mckinsey.com/industries/retail/our-insights/the-young-and-the-restless-generation-z-in-america (accessed 27 February 2022).
    Francis, T., and Hoefel, F. (2018). "True Gen": Generation Z and Its Implications for Companies. McKinsey (12 November). www.mckinsey.com/industries/retail/our-insights/cracking-the-code-on-millennial-consumers (accessed 27 February 2022).
    Finneman, B., Ivory, J., Marchessou, S., et al. (2017). Cracking the Code on Millennial Consumers. McKinsey (18 March). www.mckinsey.com/industries/consumer-packaged-goods/our-insights/true-gen-generation-z-and-its-implications-for-companies (accessed 27 February 2022).

13. *Encyclopedia Britannica*. ITT Corporation. https://www.britannica.com/topic/ITT-Corporation (accessed 15 September 2021).

14. Wang, Y, (2020). In China, The "Great Firewall'" Is Changing a Generation. *Politico* (1 September). www.politico.com/news/magazine/2020/09/01/china-great-firewall-generation-405385 (accessed 16 September 2021).

15. Kleinman, Z. (2020). What Is Tencent? *BBC News* (7 August). www.bbc.com/news/technology-53696743 (accessed 16 September 2021).
    Bischoff, P. (2014). Tencent Owns 3 of the World's 5 Biggest Social Networks. *Tech in Asia* (2 November). www.techinasia.com/tencent-owns-3-worlds-5-biggest-social-networks (accessed 17 September 2021).
    Cantale, S., and Buche, I. (2018). How Tencent Became the World's Most Valuable Social Network Firm—With Barely Any Advertising. *The Conversation* (18 January). www.theconversation.com/how-tencent-became-the-worlds-most-valuable-social-network-firm-with-barely-any-advertising-90334 (accessed 17 September 2021).

16. Sapra, B. (2019). This Chinese Super-App Is Apple's Biggest Threat in China and Could Be a Blueprint for Facebook's Future. *Business Insider* (21 December). www.businessinsider.com/chinese-superapp-wechat-best-feature-walkthrough-2019-12 (accessed 17 September 2021).

17. Cantale and Buche (2018).

18. Thomala, L.L. (2022). Number of Monthly Active Users of WeChat Mini Programs in China from September 2018 to September 2020. *Statista* (4 February). www.statista.com/statistics/1228315/china-number-of-wechat-mini-program-monthly-active-users/ (accessed 28 February 2022).
    Thomala, L.L. (2022). Number of Monthly Active Users (MAU) of the Leading Payment Apps in China as of October 2021. *Statista* (22 February). www.statista.com/statistics/1211923/china-leading-payment-apps-based-on-monthly-active-users/ (accessed 28 February 2022).

19. Hackett, R. (2020). With Trump's WeChat Ban approaching, Here Are Several Alternatives. *Fortune* (18 September). www.fortune.com/2020/09/18/wechat-ban-alternatives-imessage-signal-wickr/ (accessed 17 September 2021).

20. Stone, S., and Hartmans, A. (2021). Jack Ma Hasn't Been Seen in 2 Months after Clashing with Chinese Regulators. Here's a Look at How the Alibaba and Ant Group Founder Got Started as a Scrappy Underdog and Amassed a $50 Billion Fortune. *Business Insider* (5 January). www.businessinsider.com/inspiring-life-story-of-alibaba-founder-jack-ma-2017-2 (accessed 18 September 2021).

21. D'Onfro, J. (2014). The Remarkable Story of How Alibaba Defeated eBay in China. *Business Insider* (14 April). www.businessinsider.com/how-alibaba-defeated-ebay-in-china-2014-4?op=1#the-launch-of-taobao-coincided-almost-exactly-with-ebays-decision-to-buy-the-rest-of-eachnet-and-invest-150-million-into-the-business-27 (accessed 18 September 2021).

22. Zeng, M. (2018). Alibaba and the Future of Business. *Harvard Business Review* (September–October). www.hbr.org/2018/09/alibaba-and-the-future-of-business (accessed 18 September 2021).

23. Pranshantham, S., and Woetzel, A. (2020). 3 Lessons from Chinese Firms on Effective Digital Collaboration. *Harvard Business Review* (10 August). www.hbr.org/2020/08/3-lessons-from-chinese-firms-on-effective-digital-collaboration (accessed 18 September 2021).

24. Canales, K. (2021). Alipay Is Like a Supercharged Version of Popular US Apps like Venmo and PayPal Rolled into One, and Now President Trump Is Banning It. *Business Insider* (6 January). www.businessinsider.com/what-is-alipay-ant-group-fintech-app-china (accessed 18 September 2021).

25. Liu, C. (2020). Chinese Mini-Apps Hold Big Appeal for Businesses Hit by Virus. *Nikkei Asia* (5 May). https://asia.nikkei.com/Business/China-tech/Chinese-mini-apps-hold-big-appeal-for-businesses-hit-by-virus (accessed 11 April 2022).

    Huang, Z., and Zheng, S. (2022). Tencent's WeChat App Keeps Growing Despite Beijing Crackdown. *Bloomberg* (6 January). https://www.bloomberg.com/news/articles/2022-01-06/tencent-s-wechat-app-keeps-growing-despite-beijing-crackdown (accessed 11 April 2022).

26. Zeng (2018).

27. Miller, R. (2016). How AWS Came to Be. *TechCrunch* (2 July). www.techcrunch.com/2016/07/02/andy-jassys-brief-history-of-the-genesis-of-aws/ (accessed 19 September 2021).

28. Bishai, A. (2018). How to Optimize Cost Savings in AWS Marketplace. *Amazon AWS Marketplace Blog* (29 October). www.aws.amazon.com/blogs/awsmarketplace/how-to-optimize-cost-savings-in-aws-marketplace/ (accessed 19 September 2021).

29. Barnes, B., Sperling, N., and Weise, K. (2021). James Bond, Meet Jeff Bezos: Amazon Makes $8.45 Billion Deal for MGM. *New York Times* (26 May). www.nytimes.com/2021/05/26/business/amazon-MGM.html (accessed 20 September 2021).

30. Bensinger, G. (2016). Amazon Plans Hundreds of Brick-and-Mortar Bookstores, Mall CEO Says. *Wall Street Journal* (2 February). www.wsj.com/articles/amazon-plans-hundreds-of-brick-and-mortar-bookstores-mall-ceo-says-1454449475 (accessed 20 September 2021).

31. Wingfield, N., and de la Merced, M. (2017). Amazon to Buy Whole Foods for $13.4 Billion. *New York Times* (16 June). www.nytimes.com/2017/06/16/business/dealbook/amazon-whole-foods.html (accessed 20 September 2021).

32. Wingfield, W. (2016). Amazon Moves to Cut Checkout Line, Promoting a Grab-and-Go Experience. *New York Times* (5 December). www.nytimes.com/2016/12/05/technology/amazon-moves-to-cut-checkout-line-promoting-a-grab-and-go-experience.html (accessed 20 September 2021).

33. O'Kane, S. (2017). Tesla Motors Changes Company Name to Just Tesla. *The Verge* (1 February). www.theverge.com/2017/2/1/14470094/tesla-motors-name-change-inc-solar (accessed 21 September 2021).

CHAPTER 3

1. O'Toole, G. (2013). It's Difficult to Make Predictions, Especially about the Future. *Quote Investigator* (20 October). www.quoteinvestigator. com/2013/10/20/no-predict/ (accessed 1 March 2022).

2. Tabb, M., Gawrylewski, A., and DelViscio, J. (2021). How Does a Quantum Computer Work? *Scientific American* (7 July). www.scientificamerican. com/video/how-does-a-quantum-computer-work/ (accessed 15 October 2021).

3. Verbiest, T. (2021). Is a New Decentralized Internet, or Web 3.0, Possible? *Cointelegraph* (9 June). www.cointelegraph.com/news/is-a-new-decentralized-internet-or-web-3-0-possible (accessed 15 October 2021).

4. *New York Times*. (1970). Dr. Abraham Maslow, Founder of Humanistic Psychology, Dies. (10 June). www.nytimes.com/1970/06/10/archives/ dr-abraham-maslow-founder-of-humanistic-psychology-dies.html (accessed 15 October 2021).

5. Max-Neef, M.A., Elizalde, A., and Hopenhayn, M. (1991). *Human Scale Development: Conception, Application, and Further Reflections*. New York: The Apex Press.
   Max-Neef, M.A., Elizalde, A., and Hopenhayn, M. (1989). *Human Scale Development. Development Dialogue: A Journal of International Development* (1): 17–46. www.researchgate.net/publication/285755287_Human_ scale_development_An_option_for_the_future (accessed 15 October 2021).

6. Vanham, P. (2019). A Brief History of Globalization. World Economic Forum (17 January). www.weforum.org/agenda/2019/01/how-globalization-4-0-fits-into-the-history-of-globalization/ (accessed 16 October 2021).

7. Vanham (2019).

8. European Commission. (2015). European Parliament Adopts European Commission Proposal to Create Safer and More Innovative European Payments (8 October). www.ec.europa.eu/commission/presscorner/ detail/en/IP_15_5792 (accessed 16 October 2021).

9. Morgan Stanley. (2021). Open Banking: Is the Clock Ticking for European Banks? (12 March). www.morganstanley.com/ideas/open-banking-future-european-banks/ (accessed 16 October 2021).

10. *Climate Action Tracker*. (2021). 2100 Warming Predictions: Emissions and Expected Warming Based on Pledges and Current Policies (November). www.climateactiontracker.org/global/temperatures/ (accessed 1 March 2022).
    Boehm, S., Lebling, K., Levin, K., et al. (2021). We're Not on Track for 1.5 Degrees C. What Will It Take? *Climate Action Tracker* (28 October). www. climateactiontracker.org/blog/were-not-on-track-for-15-degrees-c-what-will-it-take/ (accessed 1 March 2022).

11. Edmond, C. (2019). Scientists Have a New Suggestion to Create More Climate-Friendly Cows. World Economic Forum (22 July). www.weforum.org/agenda/2019/07/methane-cow-beef-greenhouse-gas-prebiotic/ (accessed 17 October 2021).

12. Dolgin, E. (2020). Will Cell-Based Meat Ever Be a Dinner Staple? *Nature* (9 December). www.nature.com/articles/d41586-020-03448-1 (accessed 17 October 2021).
    Schaefer, G.O. (2018). Lab-Grown Meat: Beef for Dinner—Without Killing Animals or the Environment. *Scientific American* (14 September). www.scientificamerican.com/article/lab-grown-meat/ (accessed 17 October 2021).

13. Vincent, J. (2018). This Is When AI's Top Researchers Think Artificial General Intelligence Will Be Achieved. *The Verge* (27 November). www.theverge.com/2018/11/27/18114362/ai-artificial-general-intelligence-when-achieved-martin-ford-book (accessed 18 October 2021).

14. Robertson, A., and Peters, J. (2021). What Is the Metaverse, and Do I Have to Care? *The Verge* (4 October). www.theverge.com/22701104/metaverse-explained-fortnite-roblox-facebook-horizon (accessed 18 October 2021).

15. Allyn, B. (2021). People Are Talking about Web3. Is It the Internet of the Future or Just a Buzzword? *NPR* (21 November). www.npr.org/2021/11/21/1056988346/web3-internet-jargon-or-future-vision (accessed 3 March 2022).

16. Lockert, M. (2021). DeFi: The Peer-to-Peer Financial System Based Primarily on Ethereum. *Business Insider* (29 November 2021). www.businessinsider.com/what-is-defi (accessed 3 March 2022).

17. Jeffrey, L., and Ramachandran, V. (2021). Why Ransomware Attacks Are on the Rise—and What Can Be Done to Stop Them. *PBS* (8 July). www.pbs.org/newshour/nation/why-ransomware-attacks-are-on-the-rise-and-what-can-be-done-to-stop-them (accessed 3 March 2022).

18. Parker, J. (2021). What Is the Future of Cybersecurity? *TechRadar* (20 August). www.techradar.com/news/what-is-the-future-of-cybersecurity (accessed 3 March 2022).

19. University of Michigan. (2018). Cybersecurity in Self-Driving Cars: U-M Releases Threat Identification Tool (4 January). www.news.umich.edu/cybersecurity-in-self-driving-cars-u-m-releases-threat-identification-tool/ (accessed 3 March 2022).

20. Dontov, D. (2020). The Future of Ransomware 2.0 Attacks. *Forbes* (5 June). www.forbes.com/sites/forbesbusinesscouncil/2020/06/05/the-future-of-ransomware-2-0-attacks/?sh=4f850ced4dc9 (accessed 3 March 2022).

21. Siegel, E. (2020). No, We Still Can't Use Quantum Entanglement to Communicate Faster than Light. *Forbes* (2 January). www.forbes.com/

sites/startswithabang/2020/01/02/no-we-still-cant-use-quantum-entanglement-to-communicate-faster-than-light/?sh=65ccb99e4d5d (accessed 18 October 2021).

22. Morgan Stanley. (2020). Space: Investing in the Final Frontier (24 July). www.morganstanley.com/ideas/investing-in-space (accessed 18 October 2021).

23. Morgan Stanley. (2020).

24. Weinzierl, M., and Sarang, M. (2021). The Commercial Space Age Is Here. *Harvard Business Review* (12 February). www.hbr.org/2021/02/the-commercial-space-age-is-here (accessed 18 October 2021).

25. Elvis, M. (2021). Riches in Space. *Aeon* (2 July). www.aeon.co/essays/asteroid-mining-could-pay-for-space-exploration-and-adventure (accessed 18 October 2021).

26. Landon, J., and Schneider, E. (2017). These 5 Industries Will Be First to Do Business in Space. World Economic Forum (24 November). www.weforum.org/agenda/2017/11/industries-will-make-money-in-space/ (accessed 19 October 2021).

27. Barrangou, R. (2015). The Roles of CRISPR–Cas Systems in Adaptive Immunity and Beyond. *Current Opinion in Immunology* (32): 36–41. www.sciencedirect.com/science/article/abs/pii/S0952791514001563?via%3Dihub.

28. *New Scientist.* CRISPR: A Technology that Can Be Used to Edit Genes. https://www.newscientist.com/definition/what-is-crispr/ (accessed 19 October 2021).

29. Ravven, W. (2020). Could Gene Editing Enable Us to Reverse Some of the Ravages of Aging? *Stanford Engineering* (6 March). https://engineering.stanford.edu/magazine/article/could-gene-editing-enable-us-reverse-some-ravages-aging (accessed 17 June 2022).

30. Chui, M., Evers, M., Manyika, J., et al. (2020). The Bio Revolution: Innovations Transforming Economies, Societies, and Our Lives. McKinsey Global Institute (13 May). www.mckinsey.com/industries/life-sciences/our-insights/the-bio-revolution-innovations-transforming-economies-societies-and-our-lives (accessed 19 October 2021).

31. Boyle, L. (2020). Gene-Editing Cows Could Cut Greenhouse Gas Emissions from Their Farts and Belches, Study Suggests. *Independent* (7 October). www.independent.co.uk/climate-change/news/cows-cattle-gene-editing-climate-change-crisis-methane-emissions-b863386.html (accessed 19 October 2021).

32. Diorio-Toth, H., and Tkacik, D. (2017). Graphene Is the Future of Nanotechnology. Carnegie Mellon University (1 August). www.engineering.cmu.edu/news-events/news/2017/08/01-graphene-yang-cohen-karni.html (accessed 19 October 2021).

33. Prodromakis, T. (2016). Five Ways Nanotechnology Is Securing Your Future. *Phys.org* (22 March). www.phys.org/news/2016-03-ways-nanotechnology-future.html (accessed 19 October 2021).
34. Saini, R., Saini, S., and Sharma, S. (2010). Nanotechnology: The Future Medicine. *Journal of Cutaneous and Aesthetic Surgery* 3 (1): 32–33. www.ncbi.nlm.nih.gov/pmc/articles/PMC2890134/ (accessed 19 October 2021).

CHAPTER 4

1. Bertaut, J. (1916). *Napoleon: In His Own Words* (trans. Law, H.E. and Rhodes, C.L.) Chicago: McClurg & Co. www.archive.org/details/napoleoninhisown00napo/page/n37/mode/2up?q=two+forces (accessed 3 March 2022).
2. Mitchell, H. (2011). Steve Jobs Used Wayne Gretzky as Inspiration. *Los Angeles Times* (6 October). www.latimesblogs.latimes.com/sports_blog/2011/10/steve-jobs-used-wayne-gretzky-as-inspiration.html (accessed 11 November 2021).
3. *MIT Technology Review Insights*. (2019). Self-Driving Cars Take the Wheel (15 February). www.technologyreview.com/2019/02/15/137381/self-driving-cars-take-the-wheel/ (accessed 3 March 2022).
4. Markus, F. (2021). The EV Tech that Will Improve Range, Cost, and Environmental Impact. *Motor Trend* (14 June). www.motortrend.com/features/tech-trends-battery-fuel-cell-motors/ (accessed 3 March 2022).
5. Hartley, S., and Saunders, J. (2017). Securing the Data Center on Wheels. *Info Security* (24 August). www.infosecurity-magazine.com/opinions/securing-data-center-wheels/ (accessed 11 November 2021).
6. Taub, E. (2017). Envisioning the Car of the Future as a Living Room on Wheels. *New York Times* (15 June). www.nytimes.com/2017/06/15/automobiles/wheels/driverless-cars-interior.html (accessed 3 March 2022).
7. Fengler, W. (2020). The End of the Car as We Know It: What COVID-19 Means to Mobility in Europe. The Brookings Institution (28 September). www.brookings.edu/blog/future-development/2020/09/28/the-end-of-the-car-as-we-know-it-what-covid-19-means-to-mobility-in-europe/ (accessed 12 November 2021).
8. Barry, K. (2021). Big Bets and Broken Promises: A Timeline of Tesla's Self-Driving Aspirations. *Consumer Reports* (11 November). www.consumer-reports.org/autonomous-driving/timeline-of-tesla-self-driving-aspirations-a9686689375/ (accessed 13 November 2021).
9. Feiner, L. (2021). Alphabet's Self-Driving Car Company Waymo Announces $2.5 Billion Investment Round. *CNBC* (16 June). www.cnbc.com/2021/06/16/alphabets-waymo-raises-2point5-billion-in-new-investment-round.html (accessed 13 November 2021).

10. Gallo, C. (2021). How Jeff Bezos Consistently Communicates Four Core Values that Made Amazon a Success. *Forbes* (11 February). www.forbes.com/sites/carminegallo/2021/02/11/how-jeff-bezos-consistently-communicates-four-core-values-that-made-amazon-a-success/?sh=67d7ece06e24 (accessed 13 November 2021).

CHAPTER 5

1. Singh, M. (2021). Google Play Drops Commissions to 15% from 30%, Following Apple's Move Last Year. *TechCrunch* (16 March). www.techcrunch.com/2021/03/16/google-play-drops-commissions-to-15-from-30-following-apples-move-last-year/ (accessed 27 March 2022).
2. *Businesswire*. (2021). Leading Rideshare Companies Launch Industry Sharing Safety Program in the U.S. (11 March). www.businesswire.com/news/home/20210311005782/en/Leading-Rideshare-Companies-Launch-Industry-Sharing-Safety-Program-in-the-U.S. (accessed 27 March 2022).
3. Hoorens, V. (2011). Self-Enhancement and Superiority Biases in Social Comparison. *European Review of Social Psychology* (1): 113–139. https://doi.org/10.1080/14792779343000040.
   DeAneglis, T. (2003). Why we overestimate our competence. *American Psychological Association* 34 (2): p. 60. www.apa.org/monitor/feb03/overestimate (accessed 27 March 2022).
4. Edmonds, E. (2018). More Americans Willing to Ride in Fully Self-Driving Cars. *AAA Newsroom* (24 January). www.newsroom.aaa.com/2018/01/americans-willing-ride-fully-self-driving-cars/ (accessed 27 March 2022).

CHAPTER 6

1. Highsmith, J. (2001). Manifesto for Agile Software Development. www.agilemanifesto.org/history.html (accessed 27 March 2022).
2. Denning, S. (2016). What Is Agile? *Forbes* (13 August). www.forbes.com/sites/stevedenning/2016/08/13/what-is-agile/?sh=5ec481e226e3 (accessed 27 March 2022).
3. Tubbs, N. (2014). *Philosophy and Modern Liberal Arts Education: Freedom Is to Learn*. London: Palgrave Macmillan. p. 1.
4. Epstein, D. (2019). *Range: Why Generalists Triumph in a Specialized World*. New York: Riverhead. p. 13.
5. Rosoff, M. (2016). The Only Reason the Mac Looks Like It Does Is Because Steve Jobs Dropped in on a Course Taught by This Former Monk. *Business Insider* (8 March). www.businessinsider.com/robert-palladino-calligraphy-class-inspired-steve-jobs-2016-3 (accessed 27 March 2022).

Fox, M. (2016). Rev. Robert Palladino, Scribe Who Shaped Apple's Fonts, Dies at 83. *New York Times* (4 March). www.nytimes.com/2016/03/06/arts/design/rev-robert-palladino-83-scribe-who-shaped-apples-fonts.html?_r=0&referer= (accessed 27 March 2022).

6. Jobs, S. (2005). You've Got to Find What You Love. Speech presented for Stanford University Commencement (12 June 2005). www.news.stanford.edu/2005/06/14/jobs-061505/ (accessed 27 March 2022).

7. Dyer, J., and Gregersen, H. (2013). The Secret to Unleashing Genius. *Forbes* (14 August). www.forbes.com/sites/innovatorsdna/2013/08/14/the-secret-to-unleashing-genius/?sh=51dd5c6e361c (accessed 29 March 2022). *Forbes*. (2021). Profile: Jeff Bezos. www.forbes.com/profile/jeff-bezos/?sh=56f330051b23.

8. Sawhney, V. (2021). Why Company Culture Matters. *Harvard Business Review* (3 December). www.hbr.org/2021/12/why-company-culture-matters-our-favorite-reads (accessed 25 March 2021).

9. Majdan, K., and Wasowski, M. (2017). We Sat Down with Microsoft's CEO to Discuss the Past, Present and Future of the Company. *Business Insider* (20 April). www.businessinsider.com/satya-nadella-microsoft-ceo-qa-2017-4 (accessed 29 March 2022).

10. Tarallo, M. (2018). The Art of Servant Leadership. *Society for Human Resources Management* (17 May). www.shrm.org/resourcesandtools/hr-topics/organizational-and-employee-development/pages/the-art-of-servant-leadership.aspx (accessed 29 March 2022).

11. Greenleaf, R. (1977). *Servant Leadership: A Journey Into the Nature of Legitimate Power and Greatness*. Mahwah, NJ: Paulist.

12. Frick, D. Robert K. Greenleaf: A Short Biography. Robert K. Greenleaf Center for Servant Leadership, Seton Hall University. www.greenleaf.org/about-us/robert-k-greenleaf-biography/ (accessed 29 March 2022).

13. Pontefract, D. (2018). The Foolishness of Fail Fast, Fail Often. *Forbes* (15 September). www.forbes.com/sites/danpontefract/2018/09/15/the-foolishness-of-fail-fast-fail-often/?sh=2f3ddb6d59d9 (accessed 29 March 2022).

About the Authors

Venkat Atluri is a senior partner with McKinsey & Company, where he leads the firm's global Tech and Telecommunications practice. He partners with top executives and boards to create value through end-to-end performance transformations, programmatic mergers and acquisitions, and new business building from incubation to scale-up. He is keenly focused on the future of technology, with special emphasis on the cross-sector opportunities at the intersection of new technologies and emerging business models. He serves clients in the high-tech, media and telecommunications (TMT), advanced industries, and consumer sectors. He also has a passion for advising venture capital and private equity investors.

Venkat is a leading expert on the vast and emerging opportunities—created by the network connectivity of devices, systems, platforms, and people—and powered by software and hardware. He draws on this expertise to guide clients through the design and deployment of network and ecosystem-based businesses across sectors. A thought leader at McKinsey, Venkat is a prolific author and sought-after speaker at industry events.

He has held many leadership positions throughout his tenure at the firm. Venkat cofounded and led McKinsey's work in Internet of Things (IoT). He led the scaleup of new analytic and digital assets along with alliances and partnerships with innovators. He spearheaded tech-enabled transformations for clients in advanced industries.

Venkat also led McKinsey's efforts globally for the TMT Practice to help clients fast-track and sustain transformational impact through leadership alignment, execution support, capability building, and leadership development with a distinctive set of assets and exceptional digital-learning programs. Prior to McKinsey, Venkat held operating leadership roles at General Electric as well as product development, management, and deployment roles at 3M.

Outside of McKinsey, Venkat serves on the board of 1871—one the world's most successful start-up incubators. He is the current chairman of the board and founding board member of CurrentWater, a non-profit that seeks sustainable solutions to water challenges through innovation and collaboration, centered on efforts to develop and deploy tools, practices, and technologies to promote sustainable blue economy growth.

Miklós Dietz is a senior partner with McKinsey & Company, where he leads the firm's global Banking Strategy and Innovation team and is the managing partner of the Vancouver office. He advises private and public sector companies in designing and implementing end-to-end transformation programs, building new businesses and executing acquisition strategies. He has served over 450 companies across 40+ countries, with special focus on financial institutions, consumer-facing businesses, startups and high-growth companies, conglomerates and the public sector.

Miklós specializes in helping organizations to create long-term, transformational visions with the intention to reinvent their very business models with a cross-sectoral value creation perspective. He is especially focused on understanding capital market value trends, designing new organizational models and customer value propositions, building capabilities and helping partnership discussions. Miklós is passionate about researching global megatrends and building large-scale strategic scenarios based on data analytics and quantitative modeling, with broad economic, environmental, and social sustainability horizons.

Within McKinsey, Miklós is the founder of Panorama, a global banking solution and research center based in Budapest, Delhi and London, the co-chair of PFIC, the knowledge and expert center of the Banking Practice and a member of the firm's cross-sectoral Knowledge Council. Before moving to Canada, he was the managing partner of

McKinsey's Budapest office, where he received the Knight's Cross of the Republic of Hungary for his help in managing the implications of the Global Financial Crisis.

Prior to McKinsey, Miklós worked for Merril Lynch in New York, California, and London. He has a MPhil degree from the University of Cambridge, an MSc from the Corvinus University and a Doctor Iuris from the ELTE University. He is a CFA Charterholder.

Index

Page numbers followed by *f* refer to figures.